Karl Marx

Paul Thomas

REAKTION BOOKS

This book is dedicated to my students, from whom I have learned much

Published by Reaktion Books Ltd
33 Great Sutton Street
London EC1V 0DX, UK

www.reaktionbooks.co.uk

First published 2012

Printed and bound in Great Britain
by Bell & Bain, Glasgow

British Library Cataloguing in Publication Data
Thomas, Paul, 1943–
    Karl Marx. — (Critical lives)
    1. Marx, Karl, 1818–1883.
    2. Communists—Germany—
    Biography.
    I. Title II. Series
    335.4'092-DC23

    ISBN 978 1 86189 906 4

Contents

Karl Marx in London, 1875.

Introduction

Do you? *Do* you?
Karl Marx to H. M. Hyndman, on the latter's remark that he himself grew
more tolerant with age

Death was a money-making proposition in Victorian London. The
newer, eastern section of Highgate Cemetery in which Karl Marx
was laid to rest on 17 March 1883 – it is separated from the older,
more ornate (and funnier) western section by Swains Lane – was
often compared in Victorian times to Père Lachaise in Paris. Père
Lachaise is in general funnier than Highgate Cemetery, but it stops
being funny very abruptly once you get to the Mur des Fédérés
(Communards' Wall), where some 147 Communards (the last of
20,000 victims of the forces of 'order') were lined up and shot in
1871. People still put flowers on the wall to this very day. This point
has not been lost on the leaders of the Parti communiste français,
who have been pious – or unscrupulous – enough to carefully
situate their own funeral plots facing the wall. (This is less of a
digression than it may at first appear, since Marx too, as we shall
see, memorably commemorated a Paris Commune that was not
in truth his inspiration.) The difference between Highgate and
Père Lachaise is that the latter was, and still is, operated by the
Prefecture of Paris, whereas freehold plots in Highgate – some
of them, like Marx's, on unhallowed ground reserved for 'free-
thinkers' – were sold on the market by the London Cemetery

Company, a joint-stock enterprise set up in 1839. Highgate may thus have been an appropriate resting place for the anatomist of Victorian capitalism – an intestate, *staatenlos* exile and 'freethinker', sceptical and irreligious to the core, to whom his German-Jewish antecedents meant next to nothing.

Marx himself however meant much to those assembled around his graveside. Few in number, these were drawn from several nationalities; the proceedings were multilingual. The two wreaths laid on the coffin – others from Russia and Switzerland did not arrive in time, Marx having died on 14 March – were in the names of the editors and staff of *Der Sozialdemokrat*, a Zurich publication that was in short order to publish the fullest extant account of the funeral; and the London Communist Workers' Educational Association. Friedrich Engels (1820–1895), Marx's long-time friend and confidant, spoke at length in English; Charles Longuet (1839–1903), the husband of Marx's eldest daughter, Jenny, read (in French) messages from Peter Lavrovich Lavrov on behalf of Russian socialists, from the Marxist wing of the French Workers' Party, and from the Madrid brotherhood of the Spanish Socialist Workers' Party; and Wilhelm Liebknecht (1826–1900), a friend of Marx and Engels since 1850, spoke rather incoherently in German 'as representative of German Social Democracy'.

Engels's well-known keynote 'Speech at the Graveside of Karl Marx' was bent upon seeing to it that the name and work of his friend and guiding spirit would 'endure through the ages'. Engels's heartfelt, distraught words – 'we are what we are because of him; without him we should still be sunk in a slough of confusion' – cannot avoid raising a question that no book about Marx can afford to ignore: that of the gap between the immediate circumstances of Marx's theorizing and the ultimate effects of the theory he produced. To put the matter baldly, Marx in Sheldon Wolin's words had 'founded a new conception of politics, revolutionary in intent, proletarian in concern, and international in scope and

The gravestone of Karl and Jenny Marx – and their housekeeper Helene Demuth – in Highgate Cemetery.

organization'. Marx, we may presume, would have wished to be remembered as the founder of these, and not, as he once described himself to his daughter Laura, as 'a machine condemned to devour books and then throw them, in a changed form, on the dunghill of history'.[1]

Not too much should be made of the fact that those assembled around Marx's grave on 17 March were few in number, though the *Pall Mall Gazette* commented at the time that the extraordinary thing was that Karl Marx's death should have been allowed to pass almost unnoticed; Marx's eldest daughter Jenny's funeral – she had died at the age of 38 in January 1883 – was better attended than her father's was to be. The surviving members of Karl Marx's family had insisted that the Highgate gathering be 'without ceremony'. 'We are not people who cling to outward show', as Marx's wife Jenny – who died in 1881 – had put it. (The plinth-like monument designed by Laurence Bradshaw that today adorns Marx's (and Jenny's) resting place and that encases the original, plain memorial

The famous memorial to Marx in London's Highgate Cemetery replaced an earlier, plainer stone; commissioned by the Communist Party of Great Britain, it was sculpted by Laurence Bradshaw in 1956.

plaque was commissioned by the Communist Party of Great Britain only in the 1950s.) Engels may have exaggerated when he said that Marx would be 'revered and mourned by millions of revolutionary fellow-workers – from the mines of Siberia to California'. But his exaggeration (if indeed it was an exaggeration) was pardonable: memorials to Marx elsewhere were to be far better attended than was his interment in London.

It is the terms in which and by which Marx was to be remembered that pose the problems. Marx was commemorated from the outset not so much as the anatomist of the kind of Victorian capitalism that had made Highgate Cemetery possible, and not as the chronicler of the age that had made Marx himself possible, but as a 'revolutionist' – he was, as Engels said, 'before all else a revolutionary' – and also as a man of science, even if 'the man of science', again in Engels's words, 'was only half the man'. Obituaries were by and large to opt either for the 'revolutionist' or for 'the man of science', though Liebknecht's graveside oration ran them together (Marx, said a doubtless distraught Liebknecht, gave 'the proletariat, the party of the working people . . . the unshakeable basis of science. A revolutionary in scientific thought and scholarship as well as a revolutionary in scientific method, he reached the highest peak of scholarship, then descended to make science the common property of the people . . . Science is the liberator of the people.')

It is here that we enter contested, though not uncharted, territory. When at Marx's graveside Engels compared Marx famously and fulsomely with Darwin – 'Just as Darwin discovered the law of evolution in organic nature, so Marx discovered the law of evolution in human history' – he was among other things advancing a *version* or interpretation of Marx.[2] This may not have accorded with how Marx had thought of himself. What Engels declaimed is also an interpretation of Marx that accords ill with – and which certainly cannot be mapped on to – another common interpretation, which tells us that Marx's intellectual and political impact is all the more striking because it was *not* based on any desire to be neutral, objective and value-free. To say this is to raise a large issue to which we will return later. Suffice it for the time being to insist on the point that these are *alternative* interpretations, and that if we are to come to any sort of understanding of how Marx's life and Marx's writings – his *work* and his *works* – interpenetrate, we must come to some decision about which interpretation is the better one to adopt. They cannot both be right.

That Marx shared in a more generalized admiration of Darwin is not at issue here. Nor indeed is the fact that Marx claimed some 'scientific' status for some of his own discoveries arrived at in the course of his 'Critique of Political Economy', as we shall see. What is at issue is whether Marx thought of these discoveries as having in some way paralleled Darwin's discoveries in a very different field of study. What is also at issue, for that matter, is whether Marx had thought of himself as a (or the) Man of Science, which is the role in which Engels, Liebknecht and others were to cast him. The Marx who as a historical figure was to be colonized by something called Marxism was in large measure the creation of Engels, as indeed was Marxism itself, which became the 'historical materialism' that was to be draped in the mantle of 'scientific socialism'.

Engels, as Marx's literary executor, was after 1883 to expend a massive amount of energy recharging his friend's reputation, seeing into print writings Marx had left unpublished during his lifetime, particularly the second (1885) and third (1894) volumes of *Capital* and his earlier 'Theses on Feuerbach'. Engels also composed updated introductions to new editions of works Marx had published: *The Poverty of Philosophy, Wage Labour and Capital, Revelations Concerning the Communist Trial in Cologne, The Class Struggles in France, The Eighteenth Brumaire of Louis Bonaparte*, and *The Civil War in France*. Engels into the bargain updated earlier writings of his own (*Anti-Dühring, Socialism: Utopian and Scientific*) and saw into print several new ones: *The Peasant War in Germany* (history); *The Origin of the Family, Private Property and the State* (anthropology, like the manuscript 'Labour in the Transition from Ape to Man'); and 'Ludwig Feuerbach and the End of Classical German Philosophy', which was an early – indeed, the earliest – philosophical 'Marxology'.

Throughout these several endeavours Engels showed a penchant for publicity that Marx himself – who exhibited what some have

Friedrich Engels, Marx's great collaborator and supporter, in the early 1840s.

regarded as a weakness for overblown, turgid satires – had not always displayed. Engels's contribution to Marx's reputation was enormous, but is difficult to assess. One of the difficulties stems from the fact that there was, during Marx's lifetime, so little real theoretical collaboration between the two friends after the 1840s. Even the spirited exchange of letters between the two – an entertaining but over-mined scholarly resource – shuddered to a halt in 1870, when Engels moved from Manchester to London. Another difficulty stems from the character of Engels's own work on Marx's behalf and on his own after Marx's death. There can be little doubt that Engels effectively set his own seal on the subsequent reception of Marx's doctrines – not just among the German Social Democrats but also, perhaps less intentionally, among Russian Marxists prior to a Bolshevik Revolution in 1917 that neither he nor Marx foresaw. In both arenas Marx was remembered and commemorated very much as Engels wanted him to be.

The truth of the matter is that if Marx did indeed 'discover' a 'law of development of human history', as Engels claimed at Marx's graveside, he seems to have been remarkably reticent about expressing it. He also refrained from equating any such laws with the 'laws' of matter in motion, which were said by the later Engels (and not by Marx) to cover even the 'laws' of thought (whatever these might be). That human history and thought are but special fields of play for nature's general laws of motion and development is an idea of Engels's that appears to owe little, if anything at all, to Marx, and little, if anything, to Darwin either. Attribution apart, this is in any case an easily contestable idea, but one that nevertheless came strongly to influence Soviet dialectical materialism in the twentieth century. The extent to which Engels's Marx corresponds to Marx as a historical figure is still a vexed question. It is more than likely that Engels in his own writings, including the posthumously published *Dialectics of Nature*, departed from Marx in important respects, making of Marxism the kind of systematic materialist metaphysics that Marx, whose central concern had been the much more finite 'critique of political economy', had singularly failed to provide.

The beginning of wisdom in dealing with how Marx ought to be remembered is to cut through the filiopietism of Marx's self-proclaimed followers, the first of whom was none other than Engels, and explicitly to distinguish the Marxian from the Marxist. The trouble with the term 'Marxist' is not that it is meaningless but that it bristles with too many meanings. That none of these meanings would have been possible without Marx is both true and not very useful. Marxist beliefs or convictions may be held or promulgated by anyone who thinks or who can persuade others that they are in keeping or consistent with Marx's intellectual or political legacy; but Marx's legacy is a construct, and there are many and various ways of constructing it.

The fact remains that as Marxism in any of its variants developed, knowledge of what Marx himself had written was woefully inadequate. Today, what Marx wrote is finally becoming available in more reliable editions than ever before. Serious study of Marx is a real possibility at last. Even so, a note of caution interposes itself: the availability of many of Marx's writings is no cause for complacency. Even now the record is not about to set itself straight automatically. Records never do. Theories and doctrines do not interpret themselves. They must be interpreted. The task of severing the Marxian from the Marxist is in no sense an easy or straightforward one, and it would in any case be slavish to suggest that Marx should be given the last word on his own doctrines or, for that matter, on anything else. But there is every reason for his words to be heard. This book is undertaken not for the sake of uncovering or disinterring a pure, unsullied Marx, sufficient unto the day, whose words alone will cast confusion to the winds. It is undertaken for the sake of getting to know a theorist with whom an open-minded, constructive encounter will still remain salutary and advantageous. Jean-Paul Sartre commented that many attempts to 'go beyond' Marx necessarily end up occupying a position not ahead of but behind Marx's, because Marx's position was itself insufficiently understood, or was importunately wrested out of its own context. Sartre's admonition has not yet lost its pertinence or its poignancy; the idea of a 'Marx beyond Marxism' remains a promising one.

This is not to say that Marx's current diffusion across the academic spectrum – the academicization of Marxism – has been an unmixed blessing, for it too has to some extent left Marx himself as a historical figure high and dry. As we shall see in what follows, there is no good reason to suppose that Marx thought of himself as a kind of sibyl, dispensing timeless truths to an anxious posterity. His concerns in the first instance were more immediate and political; his writings were provoked by political events and disputes in his own day. In principle, we are today able to situate Marx's writings in context, instead of treating them as a set of disembodied maxims that admit of indiscriminate application. Yet treating Marx in context, separating the historical Marx and the Marxian from the historic Marx, who is after all a Marxist or non-Marxist construct, remains an uphill task even now. Marx produced works of considerable intellectual complexity in circumstances that now look obscure. His posthumous reputation can easily – too easily – be made to overshadow the circumstances of his life. To the extent that his reputation is distorted and out of proportion, his life too will be similarly skewed. This at root is why biographies of Marx that were sanctioned by regimes that considered themselves Marxist were notoriously reluctant to depict aspects of Marx's life and activities that might show him in an less than favourable light. Books about Marx are often harsh from the grinding of axes, and in all too many once-'official' accounts Marx emerges *couleur de rose*. Such biographical bowdlerization would generally accompany the version of Marx's doctrine that was its intellectual complement.

At another extreme, such apologetics can be abjured, and Marx absolved from the crimes that were to be committed in his name, by virtue of his supposed obscurity during his own lifetime. Maximilien Rubel and Margaret Manale, for example, splutter out the following:

> Destroyed by silence during his lifetime, Karl Marx has been posthumously victimized by an heroic myth which has harmed his work more than did the conspiracy of silence imposed by his contemporaries. The man who could have discovered the law of ideological mystification himself became the target of new efforts at mystification by his own school. While his personality is caricatured, his words are used to mask the deeds and misdeeds of modern social leaders seeking to evade personal responsibility. The doctrines Marx intended as intellectual tools for the working class in its struggle for emancipation have been transformed into political ideology to justify material exploitation and moral slavery.[3]

This indignant denunciation – there are analogues aplenty elsewhere – is by no means baseless. But it is breathless and unfocussed. Marx's words have indeed been 'used to mask the deeds and misdeeds of [those] seeking to evade personal responsibility'. But while this has been to the detriment of his reputation, and has led to misunderstandings of his doctrine, there is no reason why his concepts cannot also be used to unmask these lies and maskings. What then of the rest of Rubel's and Manale's pronunciamento? Sad to say, it largely defeats its own purpose. To demythologize Marx by rescuing him from his followers, and to deny such continuities with them as really do exist, is to run the risk of remythologizing Marx in a different way, which is far from Rubel's and Manale's intention. Yet it comes out in what they say. The notion of a conspiracy of silence during Marx's lifetime,

Das Kapital.

Kritik der politischen Oekonomie.

Von

Karl Marx.

Erster Band.

Buch I: Der Produktionsprocess des Kapitals.

Das Recht der Uebersetzung wird vorbehalten.

Hamburg
Verlag von Otto Meissner.
1867.

New-York: L. W. Schmidt. 24 Barclay-Street.

The title page from the first volume of *Capital*, the only volume published in Marx's lifetime.

in particular, is an exaggeration, as we shall see. But it raises a real problem. Another eminent commentator helps us see its dimensions by taking a seemingly favourable period in Marx's career, then using it to raise the reader's eyebrows. The publication of volume I of *Capital* in 1867 enhanced Marx's reputation, he says, by spreading it 'beyond the confines of socialist circles' for the first time. Yet even now the German-language *Capital*, like its German author, is not as widely read as Marx demonstrably wished. Again, there appeared in 1871 *The Civil War in France*, Marx's celebrated encomium on the Paris Commune. Marx was at pains to obtain the imprimatur of the General Council of the International Working Men's Association for this English-language pamphlet, the publication of which brought him considerable attention and inadvertent

18

notoriety as 'the Red Terror Doctor'. In this way, the most celebrated working-class insurrection of the nineteenth century

played an important role in bringing Marx his European fame. For the press he was the head of the omnipotent International; through the identification of the IWMA with the Paris rising the 'Marx Party' and Marx personally acquired a fame that contributed appreciably to an awakening of interest in his work among large sections of public opinion.

Yet even now the known and available corpus of his writings was in our eminent commentator Eric Hobsbawm's opinion 'exiguous': it consisted of the *Manifesto of the Communist Party* (newly republished), the first volume of *Capital* and *The Civil War in France*.[4] Nor was this 'corpus' to grow appreciably before Engels went to work after Marx's death in 1883. Marx completed little more himself, and works (other than the *Communist Manifesto*) that had gone out of print prior to 1867 were not republished during his lifetime.

Hobsbawm's point is that even at the period of maximum visibility a would-be follower of Marx would have had precious little to go on, for most of Marx's writings were no longer in print. This is a rather misleading way of posing what is a real problem. It restricts our attention to what Hobsbawm calls the 'corpus' of published writings that were still in print from 1867 till 1883. But who is to say that these were more influential than those that had fallen out of print? Marx had published a wide variety of articles in a large number of working-class journals. By doing so he had presumably reached the audience he most immediately had in mind. (It may even be the case that the first volume of *Capital* circulated among workers – just as Marx, who worked hard on the French translation to this end, very much wanted it to.) To restrict discussion to the publication history of Hobsbawm's 'corpus', then, would have the untoward effect of making Marx's reputation a twentieth-century fait accompli rather than what it was. In the nineteenth century Marx's reception was a task, a task that is still to this very day awaiting its full accomplishment, largely because of past misapprehensions.

Marx wrote voluminously, as anyone who has seen the series of Marx's and Engels's *Collected Works* on a library bookshelf can attest. He published a substantial number of articles, some more occasional than others, in a variety of different journals: in working-class publications like George Julian Harney's *The Red Republican* in Britain, in Joseph Weydemeyer's *Die Revolution* in the United States, in radical political journals like the *Rheinische Zeitung*, the *Deutsche-Brüsseler Zeitung* and the *Neue Rheinische Zeitung* in Germany, and in important newspapers like the *New York Daily Tribune*. Marx wrote *The Poverty of Philosophy* in French in order to discredit Pierre-Joseph Proudhon, who was not much known, and not much known about, outside France, his home ground; Marx wrote *Herr Vogt* in German for similar reasons, though he had to have the book published in London; and he delivered his Address on 'Wages, Price, and Profit' in English to a working-class audience, publishing it later in English for a broader working-class readership.

On the one hand, it is true that once we move beyond Hobsbawm's scholarly 'corpus', the picture becomes fuzzier and more untidy-looking. On the other, the writings that make up an admittedly confusing network of publications can be considered minor, inconsequential or as mere *pièces d'occasion* only if we take this same 'corpus' as our point of reference. Marx was, after all, making his views known through these purportedly lesser publications, and was reaching the kind of readership he most wanted to reach – socialists, revolutionists and radicals. The extent to which these writings were disseminated among workers and absorbed by them is impossible to specify with any precision, though this is true of the 'corpus' too. It would be a serious error of perspective to assume, against the available evidence, that Marx was engaged in nothing significant except composing finished works of the kind that make up Hobsbawm's 'corpus' for posterity and posterity alone.

There is of course a greater danger. The picture of Marx as simon-pure but uninfluential during his lifetime can be made, and has been made, to complement another picture – of Marx as the author of doctrines that proved authoritarian, repressive and determinist the moment anyone tried to put them into effect. Even if this picture has an uncomfortable measure of historical truth, it does not follow that repression and authoritarianism are therefore theoretically inscribed in what Marx wrote and did – though all too many political and scholarly doctrinaires have supposed otherwise. Marx was in his own lifetime accused, by anarchists and others, of having had authoritarian tendencies as a revolutionist, particularly during the period of the International, but on closer examination (as again we shall see) there seems to be very little real substance to these accusations. They can however serve as a reminder that questions about Marx are likely to be politically loaded, and that this is just as true of questions about his life and his character as of questions about his doctrine or his legacy.

How influential was Marx during his lifetime? It is fair to say that the evidence is not yet all in. There are periods, even important decades like the 1840s, when the record of Marx's life runs thin. What we have to hand is hardly indisputable and could be used – much as the group around Marx's grave in Highgate has been used – to portray Marx either as an influential editor, journalist, propagandist, political leader, organizer and theoretician, or as a minor figure, an exiled political leader with nowhere significant to stand, whose political and organizational initiatives were either stillborn or ineffective. The truth lies somewhere in between these extremes. Finding out where is not a task of purely antiquarian interest but of urgent political and scholarly moment. Marx's various forays into proletarian political organization have been regarded either as trailblazing and pioneering, as having had a premonitory character, pregnant with future possibilities; or they have been written off as having been fruitless and inconclusive. Again, the truth lies somewhere in between these extremes. Marx's role in the revolutionary wave of 1848 is still debated, to be sure; his dedication to the short-lived International Working Men's Association was genuine and heartfelt as well as frustrating, but has not often been examined in any great detail; and his contribution to the Paris Commune, contrary to what many people thought and were encouraged to think at the time, was in fact restricted to an *ex post facto* justification of its significance and promise for the development of the workers' movement.

Scholars like Sheldon Wolin and David McLellan who defend Marx – and who share my own desire not to tar him with the brush of Stalinism – tend in a sense to overcompensate, to emphasize Marx's contributions to academic inquiry, rather as though someone were going round with a collection plate seeking contributions to his upkeep or maintenance. This is not the harmless occupation it may seem. Something significant is left out if one's viewpoint is narrowed in this way. We should consider Marx's written *works* as an intellectual legacy, but not at the expense of considering his political *work*. All too frequently Marx's written works are emphasized at the expense of his work as a revolutionist, which is bracketed as having been intermittent, inconclusive and in any case much more difficult to disentangle. And all too frequently Marx's political activity is treated as a backdrop for his theoretical production. Marx's life and Marx's works are thus considered separately. His life becomes a historical trampoline for the intellectual gymnastics provoked by his works – and about these academic disputations may comfortably proceed, while sheep may safely graze nearby.

The separation in question is inappropriate, not because Marx's life and thought add up in some mysterious way to an organic, integrated, 'seamless' whole – this is a supposition with which we can, and will, safely dispense – but because there is good reason to believe that Marx, to the extent that he was able, practised what he preached. He wanted to bring together the theoretical and the practical, thought and action; he wished to be remembered as having indicated, by the example of his life as well as by his writings, the possibility that theory and practice could converge. To reiterate, he did not wish to be remembered as the dispenser of disembodied truths for which the world was not yet ready. One pointed example must suffice, for the time being, with respect to the pitfalls in supposing otherwise. David McLellan's biography of Marx claims – against the evidence, as it happens – that 'one of the main reasons why volume 1 of *Capital* was so long in appearing and why the subsequent volumes never appeared at all [in Marx's lifetime], is that Marx's time was taken up by the work forced upon him as the leading figure in the International [Working Men's Association].'[5]

'Forced upon him'? McLellan's is an 'academic' judgement if ever there was one. Whether or not it is true, as Oscar Wilde impishly put it, that the trouble with socialism is that it 'takes up too many evenings', it is not true that Marx's time-consuming work in the International was in any way 'forced upon him'. Marx took up this work freely and voluntarily, against the advice of Engels, who thought that Marx's time would have been better spent completing *Capital*. Marx disagreed for reasons he spelled out clearly, not least in various letters to Engels. Marx could claim some share in the events leading up to the formation of the International, even though he did none of the groundwork establishing it. He was invited to join the International when it was already up and running, and he accepted the invitation with alacrity. The reasons for Marx's eagerness are evident from his letters. Having long been involuntarily isolated from what he called the *wirkliche 'Kräfte'*, the real forces, of the labour movement of any country, Marx was quick to applaud an independent, non-sectarian initiative in internationalism. (In the nineteenth century working-class internationalism was by no means the dead letter it became in the twentieth, as was demonstrated by the character of the 1848 revolutionary wave – not to mention that of the 1914 Christmas truce in the trenches along the Western Front, a much more widespread military mutiny than is often believed.) From 1864 until 1872 Marx devoted a great deal of time and effort to the International because, he explained, 'it involved a matter where it was possible to do some important work'.[6]

The 'complete emancipation of the working class', to quote the first point of the Statutes of the International, which were written by Marx, was something he regarded as of paramount importance, and the political character of the International was instrumental in persuading Marx to participate as actively as he did. The International looked as if it might become the embodiment of class consciousness among workers; it might have transformed the proletariat, as an objectively determined *Klasse an sich*, or 'class in itself', into the proletariat as a self-conscious *Klasse für sich*, or 'class for itself'. Instead of being objectively defined as a group of persons sharing positions in the prevailing mode of production, that is to say, the proletariat could also become a class that defined itself as a self-conscious agent – or so Marx claimed, and hoped. (Others have considered this claim a less than plausible instance of wishful thinking.)

In any event, the work with which Marx busied himself does not divide up neatly and categorically into theoretical contributions on the one hand and practical or political activity on the other. Marx evidently regarded them as complementary and not as mutually exclusive. The International provided Marx not with a distraction but a forum. Its emergence meant that theoretical work could have some practical effect. It is easy – too easy – to be misled by Marx's unguarded remarks, in letters to Engels and others, about how busy the International was making him. Some of Marx's most important and most influential writings were composed for the sake of the International. His lectures on 'Wages, Price, and Profit', the first real popularization of his work in *Capital*, were delivered to the General Council of the International; his address 'The Civil War in France' was published with the imprimatur of the same General Council (at some cost to Marx's standing on it, as again we shall see) in very much the same way.

The first volume of *Capital* was published in 1867, we may surmise, not *despite* Marx's work in the International but *because of* what the International signified: a resurgence of working-class activity of the kind that would prove receptive to his doctrines, doctrines which would thus have some immediate effect. A calm, scholarly atmosphere did not inspire the completion of *Capital*. Quite to the contrary, its first volume was completed in the atmosphere of intensity and urgency that distinguished the 1860s from the 1850s, a decade when the workers' movement had still been licking the wounds it had sustained in 1848. What had prompted Marx to put his thoughts into shape in 1867 (*pace* David McLellan) was the period of intense political commitment and involvement that had succeeded the doldrums of the 1850s.

A later period, stretching from the de facto demise of the International in 1872 until Marx's death in 1883, may not have been a period of all the peace and quiet a scholar might desire. Marx at last had some money, but all the same had to contend with old age and sickness. The period was thus one of political inactivity and retrenchment, in the course of which Marx's theoretical output dropped off precipitously. No longer 'distracted' by the International, Marx, to all appearances, was much more distracted by the lack of the stimulus the International had heretofore provided. This is not to say that Marx stopped working. It is

The old British Museum Reading Room in Bloomsbury, where Marx researched *Capital*.

frightening how hard Marx managed to work, at this or any other period of his life. In a single year, 1873, he filled over 50 good-sized notebooks, almost 3,000 closely written pages, with notes and excerpts from books, all of which he added to the already enormous pile of manuscripts consulted for *Capital*. Yet the form taken by this prodigious volume of work betrays a marked introversion or involution. Marx failed to go through the pile of manuscripts on his desk. The 1872–83 period was theoretically barren because it was politically bleak. For Marx theory and practice did not operate at each other's expense. They rose and fell together, in tandem. The only exceptions to the overall bleakness of the 1870s are the 'Critique of the Gotha Programme', which, being politically contentious in Germany, was read by very few people in Marx's lifetime; and *Herr Adolph Wagners Lehrbuch*, a much less important text that has been read by even fewer people since Marx's death. The reasons for Marx's otherwise resounding silence have to do with political disappointment, disillusion and defeat. Marx's hopes, once they were dashed by the savagery of the repression of the Commune, were never effectively to revive. In the long term, he may have remained optimistic. In the short term, the hoped-for social transformation seemed further away than ever.

Accounts of Marx tend, by and large, to be loaded in one way or another. Some of the theoretical ones give us a Marx too prophetic, too visionary and too impractical to have had any significant effect on the political struggles and issues of his day; the less theoretical, more biographical ones no less importunately proffer a Marx who was always in the thick of things, always up to his elbows, totally committed to quotidian political practice. This latter, more 'practical' Marx could then be seen either as foreshadowing Leninism in all its elitism, voluntarism and dirigisme, or as presaging something altogether different. There seems to be an array, a menu, of possible choices, and perhaps in the greater scheme of things there really is one. But the arguments that follow in this book are based on the conviction that Marx himself as a historical figure was concerned to refigure and transcend not what was to be on offer to us today, but what was on offer to him in his own day. This book then concerns itself with how Karl Marx's *work* relates to his *works*, how his life relates to his scholarly output or intellectual and political legacy. Once we bring to bear Marx's life upon his work, and his work upon his life, what emerges is admittedly not the tidiest of pictures. We shall encounter quotidian, even ephemeral interventions or interruptions; and we shall find *pièces d'occasion* and polemics – Marx was a skilled polemicist with a taste for vicious sarcasm – and these, like some of his political manoeuvres, may not, to our eyes, display Marx at his best. But what may seem to us insignificant, ephemeral, bombastic or ad hominem seemed important at the time *to Marx*, and this book is among other things an attempt to explain or understand why this was so; an attempt, that is, to *locate* Marx in his own time and place.

1

Trier, Bonn, Berlin, Cologne, 1818–43

Karl Marx was born on 5 May 1818 in Trier in the Rhineland, the second son of Heinrich Marx (1782–1838) and Henriette Marx, née Pressburg (1787–1863). Their first son did not survive infancy; two brothers and two sisters were to succumb to tuberculosis. Karl Marx's susceptibility to the tuberculosis that ran in and through his family would suffice to get him declared unfit for military service in 1838 and 1839.

Trier was an anomaly, a constituent part of a Rhenish Prussia that even sounds wrong. As Augusta Treverorum Trier had been a northern outpost of the Roman Empire, and as Trèves it would sometimes be French thereafter. It boasted some 12,000 inhabitants in 1818, almost all of them Catholic. Goethe had characterized Trier in 1793 much as Renan was later to characterize Jerusalem: as 'having more religious buildings than any other place the same size'. Almost all these edifices (in Trier) were Catholic: the Rhineland had been little affected by the Reformation. Revolution was another matter. Being adjacent to French territory, Trier had been a refuge for aristocratic émigrés in the earlier stages of the French Revolution, only to find itself overrun by *armées révolutionnaires* once Jacques-Pierre Brissot's curdling declamation had made of the French Revolution a revolution for export.

These armies and the reforms they brought in their train were at first welcomed. The Moselle peasants and the Trier business class were suddenly freed from feudal restrictions and burdens,

Marx's birthplace in Trier, now the Museum Karl-Marx-Haus.

the intelligentsia from priestly tutelage. And there were Church properties aplenty lying compactly to hand, waiting to be divided up and sequestrated. The inhabitants of Trier duly danced around their very own Liberty tree, and sang the Marseillaise in their very own Jacobin club. Such enthusiasms soured when, under the Napoleonic Empire, earlier reforms were rescinded and recently enjoyed liberties abrogated. French armies came over time to behave like all armies of occupation, drafting young locals as cannon fodder for distant campaigns, campaigns which in turn needed to be provided for by requisitions and exactions. When the military man approaches, as George Bernard Shaw was to say, the world locks up its spoons.

By the time of Waterloo Napoleon's foes were in their turn welcomed in Trier as liberators. Even so, the Rhineland had become a bargaining chip among the victors, who proceeded at the Congress of Vienna (1815) to turn it over to Prussia. One might almost suspect that a malevolent sense of humour was at work: few German cities can have been less 'Prussian' than Trier. Trier was to prove a trouble spot for the Prussians, a running sore, a thorn in its side that happened to occupy a strategically significant position on the map. At first the Prussians tried to handle their doubtful legacy with kid gloves, or at least not to offend the Rhine-landers' religious and political sensibilities too much. The Code Napoléon remained on the books, in all essentials, and those who had appropriated Church properties were not deprived of them. The Prussian Government sent ace administrators as emissaries among its new, Catholic subjects. (One of them was the jurist Ludwig von Westphalen, who was to become Marx's father-in-law.) But hostility to Prussian occupation and annexation was wide-spread; resentment proceeded from (among many others) the mayor, the headmaster of the Gymnasium and the *Justizrat* – personages for whom the ideals of the French Revolution lived on. True to form, the Prussians reacted by tightening the screws. Even though the French occupiers had over time removed most of the civil liberties and privileges they themselves had originally granted Rhineland Jews, state service on the part of a Jew to the French was, if highly unlikely, still possible. Under the Prussians, it was quite out of the question. One of those persons now confronted with the choice of changing his faith or his occupation was Heinrich Marx. He proceeded to have himself baptized in 1817 – no great stretch, in one sense, for someone who did not take religion too seriously. According to Edgar von Westphalen, whose sister Karl Marx was to marry, Marx *père* 'knew his Voltaire and his Rousseau inside out', like 'a real eighteenth-century Frenchman'. But Heinrich Marx, like a real eighteenth-century Frenchman, also resented the Prussian bigotry that had necessitated his 'conversion', and that of his children in 1824, though Henriette Marx delayed her own baptism until her parents had died.

Heinrich Marx converted and had the rest of the family convert to Protestantism, in a city and a province that were overwhelmingly Catholic. Karl Marx attended a Gymnasium in Trier which, though (re)named after the King of Prussia, had very few pupils who were not Catholic. The Rhineland, being Catholic, was like a foreign appendage to its distant eastern occupier, Greater Prussia. The Marx family and its surviving scion, Karl, were exceptional as well as highly prominent within Trier society both for having been Jewish and for having become Protestant. But to be prominent was to be vulnerable: in 1834 Marx *père* gave speeches – as did Ludwig von Westphalen – at the Trier Casino Club in which he referred to the provincial assembly as an institution of popular representation (*Volksvertretung*). He was thenceforward a marked man. The term *Volksvertretung* was unwelcome to the point of subversiveness to the Prussian 'authorities': 'madness' and 'treason' were among the terms duly levelled at its utterance. What cannot be overstressed is how politicized the Trier of Marx's youth was. In 1848 Trier was to be the only district in the Rhineland to send a delegation to the Frankfurt Assembly made up entirely of left-wing republicans; had these not been so distinct a minority, history might have turned on a very different pivot, and we might all have been spared a great deal of grief.

The scant evidence that survives suggests that Marx was not a particularly precocious schoolboy. Even so, his 1835 graduation essay, 'Reflections of a Young Man on Choosing a Vocation', is a mature production for a seventeen-year-old, though not because it indicates the career Marx himself proposed to pursue. (The course of study he elected to take up shortly afterwards at the University of Bonn suggests that Marx at the time wished to follow in his father's footsteps and become a lawyer.) Its first paragraph skilfully condenses one of the main arguments of Rousseau's 'Second Discourse', that humans alone among animal species are able to choose how best to comply with nature's commands. The essay proceeds to make the no less Rousseauean points that ambition, should we let it mislead us, might ensure that 'we are not called to the position where we would most shine'; and that 'we cannot always choose the vocation to which we think we are called. Our social relations, to some extent, have already begun to form before we are in a position to determine them.' Questions of how great this extent was were to preoccupy Marx for some time.

> The main principle which must guide us in the selection of a vocation is the welfare of humanity, our own perfection. One should not think that these interests combat each other . . . man's nature makes it possible for him to reach his fulfillment only by working for the perfection and welfare of his society.[1]

Marx was in short order to recognize, with all due outrage, that most people, quite to the contrary, are forced into occupational slots in a Procrustean manner, no matter what they might have considered their true 'vocation' to be.

For these and other reasons it is tempting to read Marx's youthful peregrination proleptically, as though it somehow pre-determined as well as foreshadowed later developments. While this temptation should obviously be resisted, I would take some convincing that there is no connection of any kind between the Marx of 1835, aged seventeen, and the Marx of 1867, aged 49, who was to use as the motto of *Capital* '*Segui il tuo corso, e lascia dire le genti*' ('Follow your path, and let people say what they will'). Marx would construct his identity around the rejection of any society that that did not make his ideal of self-fulfilment through social improvement a reality. To quote the *Manifesto of the Communist Party* (written when Marx was 30), 'the free development of each' should be 'the condition for the free development of all'. The old socialist formula, 'From each according to his abilities, to each according to his needs', reprised in the *Manifesto*, was to be reiterated in the 'Critique of the Gotha Programme' in 1875, one of the last things Marx published.

In the 1835 essay it remains hard to see where the romanticism ends and where the commitment to progress begins. In a sketch of Marx's life that his daughter Eleanor was to write for *Die neue Zeit* shortly after his death in 1883, the Baron Ludwig von Westphalen (1770–1842) is credited with having 'filled Karl Marx with enthusiasm for the romantic school . . . while his father read Racine and Voltaire to him, the Baron read him Homer and Shakespeare, who remained his favorite authors all his life.' Ludwig von Westphalen, despite his name, was a native of Brunswick who was seconded to Trier as a government adviser with special reference to juridical questions. He duly came into professional contact with Heinrich Marx, Marx *père*, who was counsellor-at-law for the High Court of Appeal in Trier, who also practiced in the Trier County Court, and who was soon awarded the title of *Justizrat*. The Marx and von Westphalen families became close in more senses than one. Even before romance developed between Karl and Jenny von Westphalen, the Baron appears to have taken young Karl under his wing, and may have influenced his political as well as his literary development. Westphalen's political opinions were more progressive, more developed than Heinrich Marx's – he could of course afford to be less equivocal than could Heinrich Marx by virtue of his position (not to mention his religion) – and much more progressive than those of his Prussian paymasters. He appears to have interested Marx *fils* in Saint-Simonism; Marx was to reciprocate when he dedicated his 1841 doctoral dissertation to his 'dear, fatherly friend'.

In October 1835 Marx began his studies in law at Bonn. Initially he seems to have thrown himself into his studies rather importunately. By the spring of 1836, ill from overwork, he reduced his lecture

Marx as a student in Bonn in 1836, a detail from a contemporary lithograph.

course commitment from six to four. Marx subsequently involved himself in student politics, and succumbed to the usual undergraduate high jinks to the point of coming to the attention of the police – apparently as a rowdy, and not as his father had come to their attention, as a member of a suspect political organization such as the Casino Club. Surveillance by the Prussian authorities was tight, but not foolproof. Marx joined a poets' club which may well have been a front for political discussions too; such fellow members as Karl Grün (the future collaborator with Moses Hess and founder of 'true socialism') are not known for their poetic accomplishments any more than is Karl Marx for his. Even after Marx had transferred to the more serious purlieus of Berlin, where the 'wild rampaging' of his Bonn years was not repeated – Ludwig

Feuerbach said of Berlin what denizens of the US say about the University of Chicago today, that 'other universities are positively bacchanalian compared to this workhouse' – he continued to write poetry of a floridly Romantic kind. It helped, no doubt, that just before leaving for Berlin Marx had become secretly engaged to Jenny von Westphalen (1814–1881), who was to wait a biblical seven years before marrying him in June 1843.

Marx focused his other energies in Berlin much as he had in Bonn. In Bonn he had tempered his legal studies with attendance at lectures by the Romantics Schelling and Schlegel; in Berlin Karl von Savigny purveyed a Romantic interpretation of the philosophy of law, whereas Eduard Gans, from whom Marx took a course on criminal law, was a Hegelian with an avowed interest in Saint-Simon. That Gans came to displace von Savigny may have been the least of it. Always a voracious reader, Marx read far and wide in jurisprudence, as his father wished him to, and also felt compelled (in the words of a surviving Berlin letter from Marx to his father) to 'struggle with philosophy', about which his father had rather more mixed feelings. To decide that 'the idea' of law should be sought in 'reality itself' was practically to deliver oneself over to Hegelianism, Hegelianism of the kind that would be viscerally outraged by the markedly irrational structure of Prussian political and social reality. Marx described his 'struggle' to his father in some detail – as having traversed the history of German philosophy after Kant, moving through Fichte and Schelling into Hegel – the self-same Hegel who had before the 1830s ruled the philosophical roost in Germany, but whose 'grotesque and craggy melody' Marx had earlier found unappealing. Of the notes he made to himself Marx said to his father: 'this my most cherished offspring, nurtured by moonlight, delivers me into the arms of the enemy (Hegel) like a treacherous siren'.[2]

How and why, then, did Marx make himself hostage to Hegelianism at so impressionable an age? Answering this question involves taking the broader view. If Marx would later have wished to be remembered as a pre-revolutionary thinker, Hegel's political philosophy is in large measure post-Revolutionary. It concerns itself with the principles underlying (but not in the event brought to fruition by) the French Revolution, which Hegel viewed *à rebours* or retrospectively. He believed that the present can be interpreted only in light of its past, and that our thinking (Hegel's *Geist* or spirit is not really – or not altogether – a superhuman category) has a historical character, whether we acknowledge it or not. The French Revolutionaries as heirs to the Enlightenment had acted on the intuition that we act freely only in accordance with reason. This principle was given philosophical formulation by Immanuel Kant (1724–1804), to whom freedom and morality are figurable by pure, untrammelled reason. Hegel (1770–1831) by contrast distrusted 'pure' reason as a motivator, regarding it as a purely formal category lacking the substance that only 'ethical life' – that is, the customs, mores and ways of going about things that situate us in a particular time and place – can provide. The most important overlap between Hegel's thought and that of Marx, as this was to develop, is the idea that if history, rationality and 'ethical life' could be harmonized, the result would be an ethical community in which we could fulfil our own potentialities as we contribute to the well-being of society as a whole.

By the early 1840s Marx no longer believed that the idea of law could be found in the real or that Hegel had bridged the gap between what is and what ought to be. This meant that the need to do still remained on the agenda, and that if the necessary connections were to be made Hegel's political philosophy would in a sense have triumphed despite itself. Hegel's *Philosophy of Right* had succeeded in delineating not the Prussian state in particular, the Prussian state that gave it birth and even for a while an institutional setting, but the modern state in general, which did not (yet) exist in Prussia or, for that matter, anywhere else in Germany.

An engraving of the philosopher G.W.F. Hegel, whom Marx 'stood on his head'.

Hegel's *Philosophy of Right*, that is to say, had delineated and spoken up for a state that was constitutional, that embodied the rule of law and that enjoyed central representative institutions, equality before the law, freedom of the press, public juridical proceedings, trial by jury, *la carrière ouverte aux talents* and civil rights for the Jews. These were not features of the Prussian state in 1821, when Hegel's book was published. They were, rather, the warp and woof of political contestation all over Germany, Prussia prominently included. It is by brushing up against the grain of Prussian 'developments' that Hegel succeeds in delineating the character of real developments in the sharpest relief. Hegel was not posturing when he called philosophy 'its own time apprehended in thought'. His claims both acknowledge and fail to acknowledge the *differentia specifica* of the Prussian state form alongside others that were available for comparison. But Hegel's sharp-eyed appreciation of the character and significance of the separation of state and civil society, as being both unprecedented and formative of the politics of modernity, was without parallel. State and civil society as Hegel had characterized them were antithetical categories, their antithesis being a forerunner and precondition of capitalist society at large. What separates state from civil society in the *Philosophy of Right* is their differing purposes, rationales or tempers.

Even so, Hegel's speculative presentation here as elsewhere does nothing to alter the content of the separation, but simply alters the way in which it is to be thought about. Thinking about it is what Marx duly set about doing. He joined an informal Hegelian discussion group, the Doctors' Club, in Berlin, even though he was not yet a Doctor. Moses Hess was fulsome, indeed extravagant, in his praise of the new recruit once he had (in remarkably short order) been awarded his doctorate:

> a phenomenon who has made a tremendous impression on me
> . . . the greatest, perhaps the only real philosopher now living.
> Soon when he makes his début . . . he will draw the eyes of all
> Germany upon himself. Dr Marx, as my idol is called . . . will at
> last topple medieval religion and philosophy. He combines the
> most profound philosophical earnestness with the most biting
> wit. Think of Rousseau, Voltaire, Holbach, Lessing, Heine and
> Hegel fused into one – I say fused, not just lumped together –
> and you have Dr Marx.[3]

The year these words were written, 1841, was the *annus mirabilis* of the Young Hegelian ferment, the year when David Friedrich Strauss's sequel to his 1835 *Life of Jesus* finally appeared as *Christian Dogma in its Historical Development and in Conflict with Modern Science*; when Ludwig Feuerbach published *The*

Essence of Christianity; when Bruno Bauer (no less fatefully, as we are about to see) produced the first part of his *Critique of the Synoptic Gospels* along with his *Trumpet of the Last Judgment Against Hegel the Atheist and Antichrist*.

Even so, it was only after his father's death in May 1838 that Marx dedicated himself (for a while) to philosophy, hoping that the doctoral dissertation his mentor, Bruno Bauer, was urging him to get out of the way would earn him a university teaching post, preferably at Bonn where Bauer was teaching, and also allow him at last to marry the long-suffering Jenny. This plan might have been a realistic one except for the fact that Bauer, who was given to a certain impetuousness, fell foul of the Prussian authorities by publishing religious views in the aforementioned works that the authorities found unpalatable, and got himself dismissed from his lectureship in 1841.

Marx's foray into academic philosophy was brief but intense. It centres around his doctoral dissertation on 'The Difference between the Democritean and Epicurean Philosophies of Nature' – Marx's only writing that bears the direct impress of Hegel and of the Berlin Young Hegelians. There are moments, says Marx,

> when philosophy turns its eyes to the external world . . . Just as Prometheus, having stolen fire from heaven, begins to build houses and settle on the earth, so philosophy, having extended itself to the world, turns against the world of appearances. So now with the Hegelian philosophy.

Marx attributes to Hegel the power by which modern philosophy might avoid the kind of isolation and marginalization experienced by the wise man (*sophos*) of ancient Greece. The Greeks at large could not comprehend (as Hegel in the present era could) the individual and the external world as both being parts of a unified whole. Marx takes no consolation in this but remains defiant. His

'Preface' leavens Epicurus' libertarianism with Prometheus' insolence. Marx self-consciously adopts Prometheus' creed ('In a word, I detest all the gods') as his own, regarding these words as having thrown down the gauntlet 'to all the gods of heaven and earth who fail to acknowledge human consciousness as the supreme divinity'. Marx shows us that Epicurus acknowledges this defiance, while Democritus does not. Necessity to Democritus is inexorable, but to Epicurus – for whom the goal is human self-perfection, not scientific exactitude – 'necessity is an evil, but there is no necessity to live under the control of necessity. Everywhere the paths to freedom are open, are many, short and simple.'[4]

Marx's dissertation makes Young Hegelian claims not just about freedom but also about philosophy's potential for action and progress. The irony here is that while Engels and others after Marx's death in 1883 set about constructing a comprehensive 'Marxist' philosophical world-view, this task was undertaken in blithe disregard for Marx's only philosophical offering, his doctoral dissertation, which remained unread. The Marxist world-view that was to be developed by Engels and others – among whom only G. V. Plekhanov had any kind of philosophical training – is among other things plainly at variance with Marx's own sole foray into the precincts of philosophy: his dissertation, which can thus, like the *Economic and Philosophic Manuscripts* three years later, be regarded as heterodox vis-à-vis official, ortho-dox Soviet Marxism. But this is to anticipate. Suffice it to say, for present purposes, that the determinism that was to be imbricated within the materialist metaphysics of Soviet Marxism is plainly at variance with the argument of Marx's dissertation, a dissertation which distinguishes Epicurus from Democritus in order to enter the lists *against* the determinism of the latter, in order to adopt in its stead the Epicurean principle of the freedom of conscious-ness and humanity's power to influence nature without either dominating it or being dominated by it. These were themes that

Marx was to develop in his later, non-philosophical writings, as we shall see. Engels's posthumously published *Dialectics of Nature* by contrast purveys a materialism redolent of the same Democritean materialism that Marx himself had excoriated. Not to put too fine a point on it, the 'dialectical materialism' that championed Engels's 'scientific' writings was to take the form of Soviet Marxism, a quodlibet for the philosophically tone-deaf; it is clear from his dissertation alone that Marx for his part should not be counted among the philosophically tone-deaf. In this sense his famous asseveration '*Moi, je ne suis pas Marxiste*' may stand as one of his more prescient observations.[5]

The deaths of his father in 1838, and of Ludwig von Westphalen four years later, threw Marx back on himself. It is clear from Heinrich's surviving letters to Karl and from Karl's long letter of 1837 to Heinrich that father and son had been close. Over and above the not uncommon paternal admonitions, bespeaking high hopes for Karl's future, we find father and son confiding in each other to a degree I take to be unusual. Marx, who was capable of deep personal loyalties, always revered his father's memory and carried a photographic daguerrotype of his father with him wherever he went (Engels was in 1883 to place it in Marx's coffin).

Once Bruno Bauer's dismissal had put paid to Marx's academic prospects, Marx turned to liberal journalism. This was not the kind of career move that can be described (as it were) hydraulically – with one 'avenue' blocked off, another 'outlet' must be found. It is far more fruitful to consider what Young Hegelian philosophy and left-liberal journalism might have had in common. What connects them is the nature of Prussian reaction and the character of Marx's intense opposition to it. Marx was no political innocent in the 1840s; in an unfree political climate like that of Prussia in the *Vormärz* the choice to pursue philosophy was itself a political one, because free discussion could take place at the time only within philosophical precincts; here, oppositional political and intellectual life could interpenetrate and (as it were) huddle together for warmth. By extension, slippage from the philosophical to the essayistic was easy enough in principle. We have only to consider the constellation of forces that were arrayed against philosophy and journalism alike. These forces were theological as well as political; Prussia had with all due deliberation identified itself, defined itself as a Pietist Christian state. It is important to see the battle lines here: myth, irrationality, Pietism, reaction were all lined up against personal freedom and democratization, and this confrontation was at its starkest for Marx during the period leading up to 1844. While he was in Trier 'lightening the days', as Bauer put it, of the dying Ludwig von Westphalen, Marx wrote an article on 'The Latest Prussian Censorship Instruction'[6] – an instruction that had masqueraded as a loosening of the regulations. He sent his article to Arnold Ruge's *Deutsche Jahrbücher* in Dresden, but this ill-fated journal, hitherto known as the *Hallische Jahrbücher*, had been a forum for Young Hegelian speculation, and for this reason was suppressed. The banning of the *Jahrbücher*, the dismissal of Bauer, the wheeling out of retirement of the aged Schelling (1775–1854) and his seconding to the Berlin Academy to stamp out whatever embers of Hegelianism still remained – all these developments pointed in the same direction. The Prussian government was tightening the screws again. Prussian academia was no longer to be an isolated, or *the* isolated enclave or compound within which free discussion – and thus the rudiments of a free public life – might subsist. Free discussion had long been politically ineffective; it was now to become politically impermissible. Marx's article about censorship, which suggested in passing the possibility of a non-religious morality, had finally to be published in Switzerland; the only real safety valves for free discussion now lay beyond German boundaries – not just Prussian ones – as writers were rapidly finding out.

Even so, a port in the storm appeared, within Prussia (or *Rhenish Prussia*) itself. The Young Hegelian Moses Hess persuaded a group of Rhineland industrialists (at this most inauspicious of times) to finance the publication of a new journal, the *Rheinische Zeitung,* in Cologne. On its masthead was the motto 'For Politics, Commerce, and Industry'; its declared intent was the defence of the Napoleonic *Code Civil* along with the principle of equality before the law, in the hope that these would, in time, help bring about the unification of Germany. Marx, for his part, became editor of as well as contributor to the *Rheinische Zeitung* soon after its founding. If we ask why Marx made common cause with liberal industrialists in this way, and whether Marx in so doing was accommodating himself to their values, we need to consider that liberal industrialists in the Rhineland were prepared – and even felt themselves obliged – to stand their ground against Prussian absolutism, and to do so in full knowledge of the fact that in the absence of such opposition Prussian absolutism and economic laissez-faire could be made perfectly compatible. There was nothing preordained about the advent of democracy in Prussia or, by extension, in Germany at large. The danger was that Prussia might modernize under reactionary auspices; the *Zeitung*'s secular, bourgeois principles put it on a collision course with the Prussian autocracy for this very reason. Marx wrote for it an article on the debates on the freedom of the press, in the course of which he insisted that Prussians

> doubt mankind in general but canonize individuals . . . [they] demand that we should bow down before the holy image of certain privileged individuals . . . [and they] want to regard freedom not as the natural gift . . . of reason . . . [but] as merely an individual property of certain persons and social estates.[7]

An enshrinement of self-seeking among such persons and estates, 'pious self-seeking which puts personal salvation above the salvation of all', is quite compatible with reaction and repression. Antisocial egoism (as Max Stirner was to celebrate and proselitize it) had theological sanction as well as political warrant in Prussia. Marx in his 1842 'Critique of Hegel's *Philosophy of Right*' was to triangulate absolutism, private property and individualism as the three sacrosanct props of Prussian reaction – the better to line them all up in his sights and dispose of them at one and the same time. Marx in this and other essays of the early 1830s is working towards a new, post- (French) revolutionary understanding of democracy as this could be applied to German conditions. Just as, according to Spinoza, truth is the criterion for both truth and falsity, so too democracy should be the criterion for all forms of the state, even for those forms that appear to deny it. 'Democracy is the truth of monarchy; monarchy' (whatever Hegel may have thought) 'is not the truth of democracy.'[8]

Once Marx, having produced three articles for the *Zeitung* in the summer of 1842, became editor of the journal in October, an intriguing cat-and-mouse game with the censor ensued. Every move in the game contributed to the *Zeitung*'s notoriety and circulation. Subscriptions tripled between October 1842 and January 1843. The journal attracted copy from the four corners of Germany and beyond. But Marx as editor turned against the Young Hegelian *Freien* in Berlin on the grounds that their detachment from the world around them, however 'principled' it may have been, had transformed their erstwhile critical energies into self-indulgent posturing and 'bohemian' acting out. Marx's rejection of articles by members of *die Freien* did him no good at all vis-à-vis the Prussian autocracy.

Two additional articles were to do no more to endear Marx to the Prussians. As Marx himself was later to put it, looking back from the year 1859,

> in the year 1842, as editor of the *Rheinische Zeitung*, I experienced for the first time the embarrassment of having to take part in

discussions of so-called material interests. The Proceedings of the Rhenish *Landtag* on thefts of wood and parcelling of landed property, the official polemic which Herr von Schaper, then *Oberpräsident* of the Rhine province, opened against the *Rheinische Zeitung* on the conditions of the Moselle peasantry, and finally debates on free trade and protective tariffs, provided the first occasions for occupying myself with economic questions.[9]

Before the 1820s there had been in the Rhineland a feudal right to gather fallen wood for fuel; now it was proposed to give the owners of the great forests the full rights of modern property ownership, so that wood-gathering, which within living memory had been legal and customary, would be redefined and criminalized as theft. The hook on which Marx hangs the argument of his article is not so much the plight of the poor themselves as the character of the Landtag debates about their plight. He uses the power of theory to alert his readers to what is really going on (as well as what appears to be going on) in the politics of the 1840s. In the Landtag debates the particular interests of the landowners displaced the interests of the Province and those of the poor; private property triumphed over human feeling and customary rights. This is the seamy reality behind the facade of 'representative' institutions: those having economic power were using these institutions to consolidate their hold. The same note was struck in Marx's December 1842 'Defence of the Moselle Correspondent', a correspondent who had written of the distress of the winegrowing peasantry in the Moselle. The government's indifference to the plight of these winegrowers, who had fallen on hard times, had to do, Marx argued, not with the personality flaws of the debaters but with objective circumstance, with cold hard fact of the kind that limited the scope of any possible government response. The government response to Marx's article was in the event rather less limited in scope; he was summarily

Marx as Prometheus, bound to the printing press of the banned *Rheinische Zeitung*; from a contemporary lithograph, 1843. A Prussian eagle is eating his liver.

(but scarcely unexpectedly) ousted from the editorship of the *Rheinische Zeitung* in March 1843. Elsewhere in his 1859 'Preface' Marx was to indicate that at that time [prior to Marx's 1843 dismissal] when the good will 'to go further' greatly outweighed knowledge of the subject, a philosophically weak echo of French socialism and communism made itself audible in the *Rheinische Zeitung*. I declared myself against this amateurism, but frankly confessed at the same time in a dispute with the *Allgemeine Ausburger Zeitung* that my previous studies did not permit me even to venture any judgment on the content of the French tendencies. Instead, I eagerly seized on the illusion of the managers of the *Rheinische Zeitung*, who thought that by a weaker attitude on the part of the paper they could secure a remission of the death sentence passed on it, to withdraw from the public stage into the study.

The study in question was in Kreuznach, a spa not far from Trier where Jenny von Westphalen's mother had gone to live after the death of Jenny's father. As Marx wrote to Arnold Ruge in March 1843,

> As soon as we have completed the contract [setting up a new journal, the *Deutsch-Französische Jarbücher*] I want to go to Kreuznach and get married . . . I can assure you without any romanticizing that I am head over heels and altogether seriously in love. I have been engaged for over seven years and my fiancée has on my account fought the hardest of struggles

– struggles which, as we shall see, were by no means at an end (Jenny's mother's wedding present was said to be a collection of jewellery and silver plate which the Marxes were later to pawn more than once). Karl and Jenny were married in Kreuznach in June 1843; the bridegroom did not leave (for Paris) until October, by which time – Marx being Marx – he had worked on two major articles, one on Hegel's *Philosophy of Right*, the other a demolition of Bruno Bauer's dual essays on 'The Jewish Question'.

Jenny von Westphalen, Marx's wife.

But it was not until he was thus withdrawn (not for the last time) 'from the public stage into the study' that Marx, without exactly 'settling down', cast his eyes westwards. The phase of Marx's not venturing any 'judgment on the content of the French tendencies' was drawing rapidly to a close. French radical republicanism came out rather well, after all, in comparison with the parlous and drear political realities of Germany; by 1843–4 we find Marx writing that 'the day of German resurrection will be proclaimed by the crowing of the Gallic rooster'.[10] This said, French radical republicanism had more than one face to present to those – like Marx for a while – who would wish to claim its legacy. Claiming its legacy was never a simple matter. One distinct filiation stretching from the Revolution extends conspiratorially from the *cercle social* of *enragés* (Hébert, Roux, Leclerc) through 'Gracchus' Babeuf's *conspiration des égaux* and Louis-Auguste Blanqui's revolutionary *sociétés* of the 1830s, to the League of the Just, Wilhelm Weitling (1808–1871) – the first working-class socialist to write in German – and the Communist League. This filiation, along with Marx's championing of the Silesian Weavers' revolt in 1844, should serve to remind us that he has his place not just on a philosophical line stretching through Hegel and Feuerbach, but also on a line stretching through revolutionaries whose communism was beginning to attract workers. Marx's position on this line, which became that of disputing and displacing its conspiratorial notions of revolution – he was in a position to do this by 1848 – gave Marx a place to stand: it provided him with a forum from which his views could emanate and his voice be heard.

But it did none of these things immediately. First there was work to be done, work denigrating Germany and biting the hand that had failed to feed. Marx in one of his Kreuznach honeymoon writings, the 'Critique of Hegel's *Philosophy of Right*' of 1843, provides what is in effect a historical sketch of the Germany in which he grew up, along with a critical engagement with Hegel's political philosophy. Looking back from the vantage point of his autobiographical sketch of 1859, Marx was to describe himself as having been placed, before 1843, in the 'embarrassing position of having to discuss material interests'; but any embarrassment he may have felt at the time was displaced in short order by the exasperation generated by pettifogging government interference and censorship – the 'hypocrisy, stupidity [and] gross arbitrariness' that had necessitated 'bowing and scraping, dodging and hair-splitting' on the part of someone not known for his inborn sense of tact.

The disunited German nation stood, Marx argued, in an anachronistic relationship to its more advanced neighbours. This is not to say that Germany's placement was uniformly retrograde,

as was Russia's, but that the German *Sonderweg* was at best
ambiguous, characterized, that is to say, by a disjuncture between
retrogression in some respects – such as the lack of a free press
– and philosophical precosity in others. Nevertheless, an overall
pattern of retrogression was unmistakable. Economically, Germany
lagged behind the rest of Western Europe; socially, an independent,
autonomous bourgeoisie had signally failed to develop there; and
culturally, social life throughout its precincts was infected with
boorishness and philistinism. But it was German political backwardness that most interested the 25-year-old Marx. His critique
mentions rulers 'whose greatness is in inverse proportion to their
numbers': Germany in 1843 was what it had been in 1815, a confused,
tesselated mosaic of small political units with more or less reactionary governments and overlapping juristictions. The *Staatenbund*
established in 1815 consisted of 37 sovereign principalities – 21 of
which sported populations of 100,000 or fewer – along with four
free cities. It was its absolute monarchies and its unresponsive,
unrepresentative political elites that bore the main responsibility
for placing Germany 'below the level of history'. Germany, Marx
reminds us, combines 'the civilized shortcomings of the modern
world . . . with the barbaric deficiencies of the *ancien régime*',
deficiencies which philosophy prolongs by idealizing them.
Germans 'have shared in the restorations of modern nations
without ever sharing in their revolutions'. Germany 'will one day
find itself on the level of European decadence without ever having
been on the level of European emancipation'. Until then it will
find itself marooned in a kind of historical limbo. Measured by
modern political standards, the German status quo was simply
an anachronism, Germany itself 'like some raw recruit' who is
'restricted to repeating hackneyed routines that belong to the past
of other nations'.

Even so, underdevelopment was not all of a piece. It stopped
short of contaminating every aspect of intellectual life; indeed

Germany, against all the odds, had managed to outpace the modern world in the sphere of philosophy in general and of political philosophy in particular. Germany's asymmetrical involvement in the process of modernity means that the modern state gets reflected there not at the political but at the philosophical level. Marx lapses into the past tense: 'in politics the Germans thought what other nations did'. Which is to say that down-to-earth, 'empirical' investigations can never reveal anything *significant* about the German past; the emergence of the modern state may be traced – but only in verbal form, only in the utterances and representations of German, that is Hegelian, political philosophy. Germany may even have 'left behind in theory' historical stages that 'it has not yet reached in practice'. German political philosophy in this sense is replete: 'Just as the ancient peoples lived their previous history in the imagination, in mythology, so we Germans have lived our future history in thought, in philosophy', in philosophy that is then 'the ideal prolongation of German history'; the 'dream history [*Traumgeschichte*]' embodied in German philosophy is 'the only German history that stands on an equal footing with the official modern present'.

Despite this, or for this very reason, when Marx measures Germany against the French Revolution he finds it seriously lacking. German conditions are so retrograde that even their outright extirpation would not bring Germany up to date: 'If I negate the German state of affairs in 1843, then, according to the French computation of things, I am hardly in the year 1789, and still less in the focus of the present.' It is important to acknowledge what Marx was up to in presenting his argument in this way: in a clever twist, he refutes the modernity of German politics by disarmingly *acknowledging* the modernity of German philosophy. He doesn't disagree, that is to say, with the 'Hegelian' point that that modernity had manifested itself in Germany in the philosophical register. But he sees no reason to crow about this in the manner of his contemporaries. What it signifies, after all, is disjunction – a disjunction between thought and reality – 'in Germany we thought what other nations did' – and Marx regards this disjunction as proof positive of German backwardness and underdevelopment. Observers other than Marx supposed the Germans had attained speculatively what the French had gained politically, so that there was some sort of equivalence involved, an equivalence on which a unification of German speculation and French politics might eventually be effected. Marx begs to differ. 'We are', he insists, 'the philosophical contemporaries of the present without being its historical contemporaries.' This signals disjuncture from the present, disjuncture of the kind that precludes reconciliation (*Versöhnung*) instead of leading up to it. Hegel's philosophy is the signal, warrant and guarantee that modern politics appears and can appear in Germany only in the register of pure speculation.

To the extent that Marx establishes a homology or isomorphism between French politics and German thought, he does so not in order to align the two, and certainly not in order to predict their ultimate convergence. Convergence is the least likely outcome of their counterposition. Marx goes so far as to claim that the modernity of German philosophy precludes the possibility of a modern German politics because German philosophy in his opinion *compensates* and attempts to *make up for* an inadequate, deficient politics. The compensation involved here is ideological in a sense of the word 'ideology' Marx was soon to make more familiar. It bears reiterating that Marx does not deny German philosophical advancement; he simply characterizes it as a speculative compensation for shortfalls in a deficient, retrograde reality.

Marx concludes his article with words that seem not to follow from anything in the foregoing account. 'A particular class must . . . be regarded as the notorious crime of the whole society, so that emancipation from this [criminal] sphere appears as a general emancipation.' The status of the imperative 'must' is troubling here:

A class must be formed which has radical chains, a class in civil society which is not a class of civil society, a class which is the dissolution of all classes, a sphere of society which has a universal character because its sufferings are universal, and which does not claim a particular redress because the wrong which is done to it is not a particular wrong but wrong in general. There must be formed a sphere of society which claims no traditional status but only human status, a sphere which is not opposed to particular consequences but is totally opposed to all the assumptions of the German political system; a sphere, finally, which cannot emancipate itself without emancipating itself from all the other spheres of society, without, therefore, emancipating all these other spheres [themselves], which is, in short, a total loss of humanity . . . which can only redeem itself by the total redemption of humanity. This dissolution of society as a particular class, is the proletariat.[11]

But how does the proletariat possess a universal character? By virtue of its suffering? Is it suffering itself that has a redemptive character? If so, the proletariat's existence as suffering party alone would qualify it for its 'redemptive', regenerative mission. In Marx's later writings, from his Paris years onward, it is the proletariat's activity rather than its existence that is central. Here, in the 'Critique', the last shall be first, as in Matthew 20:26–27; but it shall be first not in virtue of anything its constituents do, but purely by virtue of their exemplary deprivation, which as such needs only to be proclaimed, performatively: 'When the proletariat announces the dissolution of the existing social order, it only declares the secret of its own existence, for it is the effective dissolution.' It all seems to be a matter of declamation or pronunciamento – a form of words, a *Redeweise*, a *façon de parler*. This is arguably a singularly inadequate formulation. Its inadequacy – in comparison with Marx's own, later formulations, quite apart from others' – consists in its conflation of the objective and the subjective, the passive and the active. There is the proletariat's place in society, which is objective and involuntary; and there is its consciousness and activity, which cannot be objective and involuntary in the same way, because now human intentionality is involved. Marx's early argument renders the 'universality' of the proletariat into a static, formal, even hypostatized category or formula. The point here is not to berate – or score points against – Marx, who was in the course of working his way towards something more substantive and convincing, as we are about to see. This later, fuller desideratum, which dates from Marx's period in Paris, would involve practice, intent, purpose and agency. These taken together have a premonitory character that situational placement or even suffering per se does not necessarily allow or entail. Political action cannot be reduced to social placement, as Marx himself was later to be the first to emphasize. Even if we grant the younger Marx his point that the proletariat alone could be the basis of community by virtue of the need for community it embodies, Marx himself was later to indicate, and to act on the basis of his conviction, that community cannot be built by definition or categorically, but only through action and practice.

2

Paris, 1843–5

At the end of October 1843 Karl and Jenny Marx, married at last since June, joined Arnold Ruge and the publisher Julius Fröbel in Paris. Fröbel and Ruge had had in mind a bilingual journal, the *Deutsch-Französische Jahrbücher*, but in the event every French oppositionist invited to contribute to it demurred: Lamennais, Lamartine, Considérant, Blanc (who disliked the Germans' atheism), Leroux, Cabet, Proudhon. None of these names is a household word today, but at the time they were a roster to be reckoned with, even if they were not to be reckoned with in the pages of the *Jahrbücher*. The Germans, each and every one of whom was an émigré in Paris, went ahead unilaterally, with Herwegh, Marx, Engels and Heine contributing to the double issue that appeared in February 1844. Marx (who had in the meantime contemptuously turned down an offer to edit an 'official' journal in Berlin) became co-editor of the new *Jahrbücher* along with Ruge, but appears to have done the lion's share of the work and to have rewarded himself by including not one but two of his own articles, a 'Critique of Hegel's *Philosophy of Right*' and an essay 'On "The Jewish Question"', 'The Jewish Question' being the title of an earlier article by Bruno Bauer. The year 1844 was when Marx continued the studies of the French Revolution he had started – true to form, in the course of his honeymoon with Frau Jenny – at her mother's house in Kreuznach; the year he started attending workers' meetings as well as other socialist meetings in Paris; and the year – the first of many – in which Marx, largely under the influence of Engels, immersed himself in economic analyses, the immediate upshot of all these developments being the *Economic and Philosophic Manuscripts*.

David McLellan claims, I think correctly, that 'Marx's proclamation of the key role of the proletariat' for the first time

> is a contemporary application of the analysis of the French revolution . . . when he talked of a particular social sphere's having to 'stand for the notorious crime of society as a whole so that emancipation from this sphere appears as general self-emancipation.' It was now the proletariat that could echo the words of Sièyes, 'I am nothing and I should be everything.'[1]

Where, his article in *Vorwärts* on the Silesian weavers had asked,

> could the bourgeoisie – including the scribes and the philosophers – boast of a work like [Wilhelm] Weitling's *Guarantees of Harmony and Freedom* (1849) . . . If one compares the jejeune, timid mediocrity of German political literature with the unbounded brilliance of the literary début of the German worker; if one compares the gigantic footprints of the proletariat, still in its infancy, with the diminutive traces left by the German bourgeoisie, one can prophesy a truly athletic, powerful form for the German Cinderella.[2]

To this pivoting of the proletariat were added certain heady French socialist and communist ideas that were commonplace in the Parisian circles Marx had now begun to frequent. Marx's espousal of the proletarian cause in the *Jahrbücher* raised no eyebrows here. Marx was living not on the German periphery but at the Parisian centre, at the heart of socialist thought and action; France, as in the Critique, will in the end herald the day of German resurrection, however stand-offish the French might prove for the time being.

One of the legacies left by the Germans was, however, ominous, proceeding as it did from no less a personage than Bruno Bauer, Marx's erstwhile mentor. It took the form of a distinctly unwelcome essay, 'The Jewish Question'; in challenging its arguments, Marx raises the stakes of his own by arguing not on the basis of the Prussian state with all its shortcomings, but on that of the modern state in full flower, the heir of the Enlightenment and the French Revolution, the modern state characterized, as the Prussian was not, by democracy, equality, constitutionally guaranteed individual liberty, freedom of thought and, most pointedly of all, the eradication of religious authority from the legislative process and the separation of Church and state. The reasons why Marx adopts this *point d'appui* in order to deal with a Prussian political issue soon become apparent.

There was a great deal of sympathy for Prussian and Rhineland Jews in their demand for civic equality – an equality that they had enjoyed until recently, when it was rescinded by the Prussian government. But Bruno Bauer did not share in this sympathy, on the (Hegelian) grounds that the state, not religion, was the embodiment of reason. Bauer argued that the Jews' claims to equal treatment and participation could be granted only on the basis of a secular conception of society. Therefore, Bauer concluded, the Jews should renounce their religion as a condition of receiving the political rights for which they were agitating. For his part Marx paraphrases Bauer's position quite accurately: Bauer, he says, 'demands on the one hand that the Jew should renounce Judaism, and in general that men should renounce religion, in order to be emancipated as a citizen. On the other hand he considers, and this follows logically, that the political abolition of religion is the abolition of all religion.' Bauer, that is to say, wished to use the state to combat religion, to emancipate us from religion. Marx's riposte is shrewd. Such is the hold of religion, he argues, that even the most secular state imaginable would not be able to produce secular human beings as its constituent citizens; and it certainly would not be able to free people from their servitude in civil society, this servitude being why they resort to religion for solace in the first pace. Eventually, Marx clinches the argument of his 'On "The Jewish Question"' with the claim that even the most secular modern state would retain religious credentials. To advance this argument Marx makes use of a concept he calls 'political emancipation' in the belief that the state embodies an alienation as severe as the religious alienation to which Bauer had adverted. 'Political emancipation' is to be understood as a Rousseau-inspired presupposition of the Declaration of the Rights of Man and of the Citizen of the French Revolution: that people have the right to participate politically by virtue of their very humanity. The French Revolution had signalled once and for all that people's personal attributes, characteristics and fortunes were henceforward to be politically neutral. Their right to political participation and representation is not dependent on extraneous factors such as religious faith, rank, birth, social status, wealth or membership of any social class. All such characteristics are politically irrelevant, of no account. They are of purely individual significance.

What Bauer fails to see about this shift in the character of the state is that it creates a new kind of bifurcation, a new kind of dualism between economic actor and human being. These two spheres of existence no longer involve or refer to each other at all. In feudal society, serfdom and nobility were both economic and juridical categories. But with 'political emancipation', a person is, let's say, a capitalist or a proletarian *and* a citizen. This newfound distinction, which is one of roles, bespeaks a hard-and-fast, zero-sum separation of political from socio-economic spheres of existence. 'Political emancipation' thus denotes an emancipation of the state from civil society and of civil society from the state, that is, from any prospect of the political restraint of economic activity. The state no longer so much as attempts to superintend or control what goes on in civil society, which is left to its own devices.

With 'political emancipation', religion and property become non-political categories. Distinctions based upon these will be politically irrelevant distinctions. One votes whatever one's religion happens to be; one votes freely no matter how much or how little property one happens to possess. But religion and property do not cease to exist once the state is emancipated from their imprint. Nor do they cease to count. That the state is released from their sway does not mean that people are released in anything like the same way. It is likely that religion and property will matter very much to people in the day-to-day conduct of their lives. Political emancipation has manifestly not emancipated any person from the influence of these malign agencies, or from the divisions in society they have caused and encouraged. Political emancipation has simply emancipated the state from their influence, thus rendering the state in its modern dispensation an institution that is distant, removed, remote and alien from the realm of everyday existence. In Marx's words,

the political suppression of private property not only does not abolish private property; it actually presupposes its existence. The state abolishes, after its fashion, the distinctions established by birth, social rank, education, occupation, when it declares that these are non-political distinctions, that every member of society is an equal partner in popular sovereignty, and [when it] treats all the elements which compose the real life of the nation from the standpoint of the state. But the state nonetheless allows private property, education, occupation to act after their own fashion, namely as private property, occupation, education, and to manifest their particular nature. Far from abolishing these effective differences, it only exists as far as they are presupposed; it is conscious of being a political state and it manifests its universality only in opposition to these elements . . . The perfected political state is, by its very nature, the species life of man as opposed to his material life. All the presuppositions of this egoistic life continue to exist in civil society outside the political sphere, as qualities of civil society. When the political state has attained to its full development, man leads, not only in thought, in consciousness, but in reality, a double life – celestial and terrestrial. He lives in the political community, where he regards himself as a communal being, and in civil society where he acts simply as a private individual, treats other men as means, degrades himself to the rôle of a mere means, and becomes the plaything of alien powers. The political state in relation to civil society is just as spiritual as is heaven in relation to earth . . . In the state . . . man is the imaginary member of an imaginary sovereignty, divested of his real, individual life, and infused with an unreal universality.[3]

To say this is not to deny that citizenship in the modern state may signal the conceptual emergence of community for the first time; it is to assert that this community is *purely* conceptual, and is thus compensatory too. If, as Ludwig Feuerbach had recently argued, God is the product of human powers and human creativity that is then turned back on its human creators, if, that is, people had lost control of the outcome of their own creative and imaginative faculties, then citizenship of the modern state is itself an instance of the same kind of projection – a projection of community. What is this state itself but one more instance of human creativity's turning back on its human creator, with repressive consequences? Citizenship or community – as the purported transcendence of particularism in civil society – is bound to be illusory as long as civil society in its present form persists.

> None of the supposed rights of man . . . go beyond the egoistic man, man as he is, as a member of civil society; that is, an individual separated from the community, withdrawn into himself, preoccupied with his private interest and acting in

accordance with his private caprice. Man is far from being considered, in the rights of man, a species-being; on the contrary, species-life itself – society – appears as a system that is external to the individual and as a limitation of his original independence. The only bond between men is natural necessity, need, and private interest, the preservation of their property and their egoistic persons . . . the political liberators reduce citizenship, the political community, to a mere means for preserving these so-called rights of man; and consequently . . . the citizen is declared to be the servant of the egoistic 'man' . . . the sphere in which man functions as a species-being is degraded to a level beneath the sphere where he functions as a partial being, and, finally . . . it is man as a bourgeois and not man as a citizen who is considered the true and authentic man.[4]

The state masquerades as the communal as it masks, conceals and protects particular economic interests. Since the state compensates people by providing an illusory communal life, it should be awarded religious credentials, no matter how secular the modern state may be.

Bruno Bauer stands exposed. He took himself to be offering a secular solution to a religious problem, but in reality he offered a religious solution to a secular problem. With the emergence of the modern state, to reiterate, universal suffrage frees the state from the direct domination of wealth, but does not free people from its influence. Instead, wealth and property are themselves freed; they become less constrained than ever. The parallel, again, is with religion. The state is set free from religion with the separation of Church and state. But people are not set free in anything like the same way. The secular state does nothing to free them from the hold of religion. Indeed, it becomes religious in its own right.

Political emancipation is a reduction of man, on the one hand to a member of civil society, an independent and egoistic individual, and on the other hand, to a citizen, to a moral person. Human emancipation will only be complete when the real, individual man has absorbed into himself the abstract citizen; when as an individual man, in his everyday life, in his work, and in his relationships, he has become a species-being; and when he has recognized and organized his own powers (*forces propres*) as social powers so that he no longer separates this social power from himself as political power.[5]

How though do these counterposed categories, political emancipation and human emancipation, relate? They are not antithetical: political amounts not to a denial of human emancipation but to an incomplete stage of it. Bauer took the part for the whole, the abstract for the concrete, the illusion for the reality. All the more reason for us not to make the same mistake. Political emancipation is in reality a presentiment. It blazes the trail of human emancipation. But if it presages and prefigures human emancipation, it also parodies it. Political emancipation in a sense is a cruel joke on mankind, mocking the commonality we all increasingly need. It withholds, it denies, as it promises emancipation in its true measure.

Five years later, in the *Manifesto of the Communist Party* we shall find Marx observing that while modern civil society claims to be able to put the material world at the disposal of mankind, it ends up putting humanity at the disposal of the material process of production. There is more than a hint of this in 'On "The Jewish Question"', where citizenship appears as a universal category, but awaits its substantiation or fulfilment. Political emancipation signals the real, human emancipation towards which it tends or gestures; but it also makes people 'the playthings of alien powers', powers which can only stifle the 'universal' side of our nature or 'species-being'.

The Prussian authorities were aghast at the appearance of the *Deutsch-französische Jahrbücher*. In April 1844 they informed the provincial authorities that the journal fell within the definition of attempted high treason and *lèse-majesté*; the police were instructed to place Ruge, Marx, Heine, Bernays and their collaborators under arrest should any of these be so importunate as to set foot on Prussian soil. Not to be outdone, the head of the Austrian police and censorship department described the *Deutsch-französische Jahrbücher* as a publication 'whose loathsome and disgusting contents surpass everything previously published by the revolutionary press'. Booksellers in Prussia were 'notified of the severe penalties involved' in stocking or selling it, and bookshops were searched.

We have no way of knowing how much *succès de scandale* the journal enjoyed despite, or because of, these official reactions. What we do know is that Jenny Marx took her first daughter, also named Jenny, at the age of one month to Kreuznach in June 1844 (little Jenny's life was saved in Paris, according to family legend, by the exiled poet Heinrich Heine). We know also that back in Paris Fröbel buckled under Prussian threats, got cold feet and withdrew his

A romanticized depiction of Marx editing the *Deutsch-französische Jahrbücher*; Engels is looking over his shoulder.

backing from the *Jahrbücher*, and that Ruge, claiming (falsely) to be hard up and pressed for cash, felt disinclined to continue without him. Marx was left in the lurch, with nothing to his name except some unsold copies. Under these circumstances it is perhaps unsurprising that Marx and Ruge began to diverge politically as well as personally. Marx attacked an article Ruge had written in *Vorwärts*, which after the suppression of the *Jahrbücher* was the only radical German-language journal published in Paris (or indeed anywhere in Europe – these were trying times). Ruge had argued that no social revolt could ever succeed in Germany because political consciousness there was so extremely underdeveloped. Marx in his response, 'The King of Prussia and Social Reform', favourably compared the revolt of the Silesian weavers (1844) with workers' revolts in France and England, on the grounds, following from the arguments of his two *Jahrbücher* articles, that whereas the English and the French may have shown political consciousness, the Silesians showed something more developed: class consciousness. This, Marx thought, shows that

> the German proletariat is the theorist of the European proletariat, just as the English proletariat is its economist and the French proletariat its politician . . . Germany, though incapable of political revolution, has a classical summons to social revolution . . . Only in social revolution can a philosophical people find its suitable practice.

These formulations, while they fail to demolish Ruge's admittedly more prosaic argument, certainly point Marx in the direction of the *Manifesto of the Communist Party*:

> a social revolution involves the standpoint of the whole because it is a protest of men against dehumanized life even if it occurs in only one factory district, because it proceeds from the standpoint

of the single actual individual, because the community against whose separation from himself the individual reacts is the true community of man, human existence. The political soul of a revolution, on the other hand, consists in the tendency of politically influential classes to end their isolation from the state and from power. Its standpoint is that of the state, an abstract whole, which exists only through the separation from actual life which is unthinkable without the organized antithesis between the universal idea and the individual existence of man.

Ruge had thought that social revolution needs political consciousness; Marx thinks it needs social consciousness:

Any revolution breaks up the old society; to that extent it is social. Any revolution overthrows the old ruling power; to that extent it is political . . . Revolution in general – the overthrow of the existing ruling power and the dissolution of the old conditions – is a political act. Without revolution, however, socialism cannot come about. It requires this political act so far as it needs overthrow and dissolution. But where its organizing activity begins, where its own aim and spirit emerge, there socialism throws the political hull away.[6]

As a characterization of the Silesian weavers Marx's picture, like Heine's in his 'Weavers' Song', is overdrawn (they were artisans, not proletarians, and could hardly have been anything else), and the idea that 'organizing activity' dispenses with politics betrays a constricted view of what politics is, or what politics can or could be. But whatever its drawbacks – Marx might have been seething with righteous indignation against Ruge when he wrote it – 'The King of Prussia' is one buckle or link between Marx's German articles and the *Manifesto of the Communist Party*; and the *Economic and Philosophic Manuscripts* are another.

The Economic and Philosophic Manuscripts

Marx began a systematic study of political economy in April 1844, reading Proudhon's first and second *Mémoires sur la propriété* along with works by Adam Smith, David Ricardo, James Mill, John Ramsay MacCulloch, Lord Lauderdale, Jean-Baptiste Say, Simonde de Sismondi, Constantin Pecqueur, Skarbek, Cherbuliez, Child, Destutt de Tracy and others. Marx's excerpt notes and critical comments on James Mill have survived, and it is clear from these and from the *Economic and Philosophic Manuscripts* of 1844 that Marx's 'Critique of Political Economy', his life's work, was now well under way. So indeed were his working methods: he would often – too often – leave writings unfinished in order (in Arnold Ruge's words) to 'plunge time and again into an endless sea of books'. Engels, who had also contributed to the *Jahrbücher* and to *Vorwärts*, and who was engaged in writing his *Condition of the Working Class in England*, visited Marx in Paris in August. He too was eager that Marx pursue his economic studies, and may well have acted as a catalyst.

First and foremost, Marx wishes in his *Manuscripts* to establish that there is something qualitatively new about the capitalist process of production. It is not just that more goods get produced more efficiently, or that more workers, concentrated together in larger productive units, are involved in the production of these goods. These would be quantitative changes, and while these have taken place and continue to do so, they cannot tell the whole story: Marx is also pointing to a difference in character, a difference in kind and not just a difference of degree. The producer under capitalist conditions has a qualitatively new relation to what he produces and how he produces it. The individual producer has lost any control his precursor might have exercised over the end product of his labour. And while in one sense some sort of loss obtains whenever anyone anywhere has made anything, this is not the sense that preoccupies Marx. Any object produced at any time will be endowed with a separate existence, and will to this extent stand apart from the person who produced it. In any act of production, that is to say, labour gets expressed as or congealed into an object, a product that is then separate from and external to its producer. The object will be a manifestation, a residue or a trace of the labour expended in its production. But this is only part of what Marx has in mind, because the object produced under capitalist conditions will exist not just apart from its producer, along an axis of separation. It will also stand opposed to its producer. It is no longer just separate from, or exterior to its producer, but now newly remote, foreign, hostile and inimical to this same producer.

In what, then, does this newfound enmity (or *Vergegenständlichung*) consist? The product, to begin with, is unrelated to whatever specific skills, aptitudes, talents or preferences the individual worker may possess or display. It has ceased to be the objective embodiment of the individual worker's own, human distinctiveness. Marx is suggesting not that pre-capitalist production was nothing but craftsmanship writ large, but that under the conditions of standardized mass production that capitalism inaugurates there can be nothing distinctive about the product of labour as such at all. It bears no individual imprint, profile or 'signature'; no matter who produces it, it will look the same and be the same. The worker did not choose whether to make it. He was directed to do so. He did not choose how to make it. That decision is not his to make, and has been removed, or forcibly wrested, from him. The worker is certainly not free to choose *not* to produce various objects in a certain specified manner, even if he has no use for such things. He is required to produce certain objects in a certain manner in order to secure the necessities of life.

Once the object is produced, it is not up to the worker to decide what to do with it – whether to use (or 'consume') it or to transfer it to someone else, and if so to whom it should be transferred and on what terms. These decisions too are made for him – in his stead, but not on his behalf. All these various, serial deprivations are losses of control; all of them are involved in the designation of the object produced under capitalist conditions as a 'commodity'; and all involve what Marx regards as a 'commodification' of the worker himself, even though Marx had not yet come up with the concept of 'labour power' which would later clinch this aspect of his argument. At every stage of a commodity's conceptualization, manufacture, distribution, exchange and consumption, the commodity can no longer realistically be said to bear any relationship to the worker who produces it, and, to this extent, the worker becomes an instrument of its production – which is to say that with the onset of capitalism a severe reversal of the most basic priorities has set in.

The product is 'alien' to the producer, to recapitulate, not simply in the sense of being unfulfilling to, and standing apart or separately from, the producer, but also alien in the more active sense of being positively detrimental to his well-being. The product, that is to say, 'stands opposed to' the producer as a power over this producer; production deadens and dehumanizes the living worker, and gives life and form to whatever this producer produces, which then becomes actively hostile to him. Production properly so-called is however not an act but a process, particularly under capitalist conditions.

Till now we have been considering the estrangement, the alienation of the worker in only one of its aspects, i.e., the worker's relationship to the products of his labour. But the estrangement is manifested not only in the result, but in the act of production – within the producing activity itself. How would the worker come to face the product of his activity as a stranger, were it not that in the very act of production he was estranging himself from himself? The product is after all but the summary of the activity of production. If then the product of labour is alienation, production itself must be active alienation, the alienation of activity, the activity of alienation. In the estrangement of the object of labour is merely summarized the estrangement, the alienation, in the activity of labour itself.[7]

To the extent that the productive process is reduced to a series of standardized operations, involving the rote repetition of set actions, the worker will feel not fulfilled but denied in the activity of working, and this feeling will be an accurate appraisal on the worker's part of the work he is constrained to undertake; he will view his own activity as an 'alien activity', he will feel his work to be demeaning, a constraint, and it will be avoided whenever circumstances allow. If, as in the 'normal' course of events, it cannot be avoided, the worker will not feel 'at home' or at one with himself (*bei sich*) while he is under the constraint of working. This point strikes deeper than might initially be supposed. Humanity as a species possesses the capacity to render the natural world, or aspects of the natural world, congruent with its needs by means of working on it. It is not just that while mankind is one of a number of animal species that make things, mankind is the only animal species whose survival depends on the things he has made; it strikes deeper than this. As Marx put the matter in the first volume of *Capital*, in words that are strikingly congruent with what he had said in the 1844 *Manuscripts*,

labour is first of all a process between man and nature, a process by which man through his own actions mediates, regulates and controls the metabolism between himself and nature. He confronts the material of nature as a force of nature. He sets in motion the natural forces which belong to his own body, his arms, legs, head and hands, in order to appropriate the materials of nature in a form suited to his own needs.[8]

Other animal species also confront the materials of nature and turn them to account in what appears to be a broadly similar manner; but what distinguishes human work from that of other natural species is its free, conscious character.

> The animal is immediately identical with its life-activity. It does not distinguish itself from it. It is its life-activity. Man makes his life-activity itself the object of his will and consciousness. He has a conscious life-activity. It is not a determination with which he directly merges. Conscious life-activity directly distinguishes man from animal life-activity.[9]

What makes human labour human also and by the same token makes it natural; human needs and our means of satisfying them are no different in principle from those of any other natural species. Our hands, organs, dimensions, senses and passions are all prima facie natural characteristics as well as distinctively human ones.

Marx's point is not that people necessarily or always apply themselves to nature in a natural way. It is that in principle we can do so. If our labour is in this way a natural force, it is possible to distinguish human labour from the logic of animal behaviour and survival by virtue of its conscious, intentional force, and this is what Marx sets about doing.

> The universality of man is, in practice, manifested precisely in the universality which makes all nature his inorganic body – both inasmuch as nature is . . . his direct means of life and . . . the material, the object, and the instrument of his life-activity . . . Man lives on nature . . . nature is his body, with which he must remain in continuous interaction if he is not to die.[10]

When we labour, turning the rest of nature to account, we affirm ourselves as a species; we develop our physical and mental energies; we experience ourselves and begin to feel conscious of ourselves. We are acting, or can act, freely and spontaneously, without any

A page from Marx's almost illegible notebooks, including parts of the 'Theses On Feuerbach'. The concluding Eleventh, to be quoted on Marx's memorial, famously reads: 'The philosophers have only *interpreted* the world in various ways; the point however is to *change* it.'

non-biological external compulsion. These characteristics of human labour are natural to us as a species. The human features of our labour, that is to say, do not deny but affirm our natural status, even though none of them can be said to characterize animal behaviour even of a learned instinctive kind. Types of behaviour that human beings share with members of other animal species ('eating, drinking, procreating'), once they become 'sole and ultimate ends' of human existence, turn into animal functions that Marx thinks unnatural for us, though they would not be unnatural as 'sole and ultimate ends' for other species. Marx's indictment of capitalism and the alien labour that supports it is that it inverts our relationship with nature by making means of life like 'eating, drinking, procreating' appear as the goals of each and every act of labour we undertake. If, as Marx says, 'what is animal becomes human and what is human becomes animal', this is a historically specific reversal of natural priorities for which capitalism and its defenders are to be roundly indicted.

It is a reversal with far-reaching implications. If labour under capitalist conditions becomes a necessary evil, undertaken because of the compulsion of direct physical needs, the distinction between 'work' on the one hand and 'leisure' on the other will become unquestioned and taken for granted, though it is in no way a natural distinction. It is a bogus distinction, not because Marx indicates its ersatz character, but because many if not most people have the experience at one time or another of working very hard at a project of their own choosing, and of deriving satisfaction and happiness from the experience of doing so. The point then is to make such satisfaction less exceptional, more expectable. And if labour is in the meantime experienced as the activity of working under hostile conditions, we need to question the character, the source, of this same hostility. Marx sometimes in the *Manuscripts* attributes hostility to the object produced, sometimes to the capitalist who owns the productive process, controls it, has disposition over it or profits from it. But these are only partial explanations. The source of the hostility experienced by the worker lies not in the product, not in the process of its production and not in the capitalist, for all these are expressions or manifestations of something more fundamental: the powers that dominate both production and the functions of the capitalist, the impersonal rules that govern the productive process and the actions of the capitalist alike. Marx was to use the *Manuscripts* as a kind of palimpsest for the following sentences in *The Holy Family*:

> The propertied class and the class of the proletariat represent the same human self-alienation. But the former feels comfortable and self-confirmed in this alienation, knowing that this alienation is its own power and possessing in it the semblance of a human existence. The latter feels itself ruined in this alienation.[11]

It is the productive process of society as a whole that produces and reproduces the conditions of alienated labour. It is the profile of the market mechanism, not that of the individual worker or even the individual capitalist, that is reflected at the level of any act of individual production. The more commodities get produced, the stronger will be the power of the market mechanism operating to the detriment of the individual producer. The 1844 *Manuscripts* open with the following generalization:

> The worker becomes all the poorer the more wealth he produces, the more his production increases in power and range. The worker becomes an ever cheaper commodity the more commodities he creates. With the increasing value of the world of things proceeds in direct proportion the devaluation of the world of men.[12]

The proletarian in, by and through his work produces and reproduces capital, and himself as the producer of commodities. Labour by its very nature generates something beyond itself even under the most alienating of conditions; labour, under capitalism, produces and constantly reproduces the power by which the labourer's further exploitation is made possible. To the extent that our history is the record of human activity, of purposive transformation of the world around us, we have now, with the onset and persistence of capitalism, lost control of this activity and of its very preconditions. People now enter into the making of history as private individuals whose actions have consequences that are independent of their will and intentions, so that the humblest production of the necessities of life confronts them as an alien act. Such confrontation is however experienced, not just registered, by its victims; capitalism brings workers together in larger productive units, so that opposition to such unwelcome developments, opposition that will take the form of association from below, and not co-ordination according to the logic of production, is both possible in principle and likely in practice. The chain of causality can in principle be broken; alienation is not escape-proof provided that the worker become 'misery conscious of his misery', and not just aware that he is miserable, and provided that the worker can take action on his own behalf and on behalf of others like him. 'Can' does not mean 'will', but already in the *Manuscripts* Marx is locating himself as a theorist on the cusp of the difference between the two.

Marx's argument has to it a specificity and an originality that had been lacking in earlier ones – even in his own earlier ones. True, Saint-Just had proclaimed that *les malheureux sont la puissance de la terre*; and Rousseau's hatred of inequality – to give another prominent example – was visceral. Even so, it was cast in quantitative terms of wealth versus poverty. Questions about the sources of wealth, about the changing ways in which wealth was generated, accumulated and concentrated in the hands of the few, and how these few were themselves to be characterized – these were not questions within Rousseau's remit. But they most certainly were within Marx's. Marx was concerned to trace out what were qualitative as well as quantitative shifts. At the bottom of the heap we find not 'the poor' whom you 'have always with you', but the proletarian, forcibly severed from ownership of the means of production and alienated from the productive process at large. The proletarian is in this way a very different and much more specific category than 'the labouring poor' in general had long remained. The proletarian is exemplar and paradigm of loss of control over the conditions of existence, and has emerged as such because productive relationships in society, and not just the amounts of wealth held within it, have become the units of analysis. Capitalism's lineaments are susceptible to a historical and economic tracing out. The emergence and persistence of capitalism as something qualitatively as well as quantitatively new can now be explained, accounted for – and superseded.

Again, 'can' does not mean 'will', but the reasons for the unsettling social and political changes that were calling forth discontent may now be explained theoretically, and explained in such a way that the theory involved in this explanation will (directly or indirectly) stimulate change of the appropriate kind. Theory, once it is geared to revolutionary change in this way, cannot *create* resentment, dissatisfaction and the desire for fundamental change. What it can and should do is *inform* this discontent, channel and steer it into worthwhile directions. The proletarian is premonition as well as victim. What theory can bring forth is the paradoxical marginality and centrality of the proletariat's position in society, as not just one group among others, jostling with them for some supposed supremacy, but instead as a class that is outside the exchange system in that none of the benefits of the latter accrue to it. The proletarians are excluded by virtue of their marginality as well as by their poverty and alienation. The proletariat is liminal, outside the exchange system even though or precisely because the labour of its constituent members plays a key part in the maintenance of this same system. Marx's arguments in the *Manuscripts* and beyond are double-barrelled. On the one hand, the *Manuscripts*, the *Grundrisse* and *Capital* all seek to document and account for the metamorphosis of human relationships into phenomena of the market, to examine in detail the alienating effects of the progressive development of capitalism, and to show how the universalization of social relationships that bourgeois society has achieved is accomplished only by the transmutation of human relationships into class relationships of a certain type. On the other, these same works, and others like them, are designed to show that without the kind of labour the proletarians are constrained to expend and exert, the system could not persist. The conditions of life and work for the proletarian are such that the basis for community and commonality among proletarians can be built only outside and against the nexus, the logic of exchange relationships. Association must of necessity proceed among the workers from below and at no-one else's behest; otherwise it will be foreclosed or short-circuited from above. If such association can be geared to revolutionary change, a fundamental recasting of human relationships will have been effected.

3

Brussels, 1845–9

In January 1845 the French Foreign Minister (and lifelong foe of republicanism and democracy) François Guizot (1787–1874) was urged by the Prussians to order the expulsion from France of all contributors to *Vorwärts* (in which Marx's essay on the Silesian weavers' revolt had appeared in 1844). Its editor, Ferdinand Cölestin Bernays, was imprisoned. Marx reluctantly left Paris in February 1845 for the closest possible refuge from the long arm of the French and German state machinery. Before he left for Brussels – where his wife Jenny, their one-year-old daughter of the same name and Friedrich Engels were soon to join him – Marx was offered a contract and an advance by the publisher Herman Leske for a book, *A Critique of Political Economy*, which was started but never completed. Arnold Ruge was not alone in having perceived a pattern here; he had written about Marx in 1844 that he

> reads . . . much; he works with uncommon intensity, and has a critical talent that sometimes degenerates into arrogant dialectics; but he finishes nothing, he breaks everything off and always plunges himself anew into an endless sea of books. By his learned disposition he belongs completely to the German world, and by his revolutionary manner of thinking, he is excluded from it.[1]

The house in the rue de l'Alliance, Brussels, in which Marx and family lived for a year, 1845–6.

What got in the way of the completion of the book this time around were further polemical attacks on the Young Hegelians – in *The Holy Family* (which Marx and Engels finished and sent off to be published before Marx left Paris), and in the more familiar *German Ideology*. The latter was occasioned by the appearance of the third volume of *Wigands Vierteljahresschrift* (1845), which contained articles by Edgar Bauer and Max Stirner, articles which indicated to Marx and Engels that speculative philosophy still needed to be vanquished, once and for all. The two of them discussed this necessity loudly and at length every night, according to Frau Jenny, and kept the entire household awake. The household thus disturbed now included a second daughter, Laura (born in September 1845), and a son, Edgar (born in December 1846).

Owing to the vagaries of its publication history, which cannot be entered into here, *The German Ideology* by Marx and Engels is often mischaracterized as having centred on Feuerbach, even though the extant manuscript says very little about Feuerbach and a great deal more about Stirner in particular. Against Stirner Marx launches the same kind of polemical attack as he had levelled at Bruno Bauer in 1843, though Stirner is dealt with at much greater length; in each case, that is to say, the polemic is not just polemic and oversteps the bounds of polemic. Marx's scorn and derision were well-judged. Here as elsewhere, he chose his targets with some care. In Michel Foucault's words, 'polemics defines alliances, recruits partisans, unites interests or opinions, represents a party; it establishes the other as an enemy, an upholder of established interests, against which one must fight until . . . this enemy is defeated.'

Marx in person was nothing if not prepossessing. Carl Schurz was to characterize the impression this exiled firebrand made on him a couple of years later:

> Marx was thirty years old and already the recognized head of a school of socialism. A thick-set, powerful man, with his high forehead, his pitch-black hair and beard, and his dark, flashing eyes, he immediately attracted general attention. He had the reputation of great learning in his subject, and what he said was in fact solid, logical and clear.[2]

Lest it be thought that Schurz was bending over backwards in his approval, he also called attention to Marx's sometimes overbearing arrogance, adding that he would never forget the biting contempt with which Marx would pronounce the word 'bourgeois'. Marx's sarcastic wit could be mordant and heavy handed in a 'Germanic' kind of way, but for all its Germanic ponderousness there can be a serrated sharpness to it as well. (One section heading in particular, sported with some panache by *The German Ideology* – '"Stirner"

Blissfully Satisfied with his Construction' – is hard to beat.) Some of *Capital*'s long footnotes are classics of the form. But of Marx's ad hominem forays into nineteenth-century French affairs, forays which unlike *The German Ideology* did find a publisher, *La Misère de la philosophie* singularly failed to dislodge Proudhon from his position of prominence as a theorist, and *The Eighteenth Brumaire of Louis Bonaparte* (a masterpiece of polemic if ever there was one) failed to dislodge Louis-Napoléon from his position as autocrat. In either case, more's the pity – not just for Marx, but for history.

Marx's foundational distinction between a *Klasse an sich*, or class in itself, and a *Klasse für sich*, or class for itself, a distinction that was first formulated in *The Poverty of Philosophy* and used, later, to memorable effect in *The Eighteenth Brumaire of Louis Bonaparte*, follows from the analysis proffered in the unpublished *German Ideology* of 1845. As we have seen, *The German Ideology* has frequently been mischaracterized as having been centred on Feuerbach, even though the section titled 'Feuerbach', which is the first section in all extant editions with pretensions to comprehensiveness, was the last to be written. In fact Marx's animus throughout *The German Ideology* was directed not so much against Feuerbach as against the 'Leipzig Council', that is to say against Bruno and Edgar Bauer and, most particularly, against the individualist anarchism of Max Stirner. These are the figures, as Marx archly put it, who confused the *theatrum mundi* with the Leipzig Book Fair; Feuerbach for his part was guilty of no such confusion. That part of *The German Ideology* that has come down to us as 'Feuerbach' is a troublesome text in that the arguments it proffers are disjointed and fragmentary. The argument fails to flow as smoothly as that of the *Economic and Philosophic Manuscripts* of 1844, even though these latter were never even intended for publication. Even so, among the fragments that make up 'Feuerbach' there are startling passages, all of them continuous in one way or another with those we can encounter in the *Manuscripts*.

An extract from the 1845 collaboration between Marx and Engels, *The German Ideology*; unpublished in their lifetimes, the manuscript was 'abandoned to the gnawing criticism of mice', as Marx put it in a later letter.

But Marx's insights in *The German Ideology* do not repeat much material that was in the *Manuscripts* because, as we have seen, Marx's aim in the later work was to demolish the residual Young Hegelian claims that continued to emanate from the 'Leipzig Council'. Marx resorted to and made use of the term 'ideology' as a figure of abuse or derision characterizing the naive form of philosophical idealism that he found in the Bauers, Grün and Stirner, all of whom believed, according to Marx, that social problems reside in abstract ideas and consequently that solutions to these problems would themselves be philosophical. To believe this was to put the cart before the horse, to dislodge and undercut practical activities in the realm of 'real life', a realm that has an obvious priority over thought.

> In direct contrast to German philosophy, which descends from heaven to earth, here it is a matter of ascending from earth to heaven. That is to say, not of setting out from what men say, imagine, conceive, not from men as narrated, thought of, imagined, conceived, in order to arrive at men in the flesh; but setting out from real, active men, and on the basis of their real life process demonstrating the development of ideological reflexes and echoes of this life process.[3]

It is a point of some importance that by 1845, when Marx and Engels started work in Brussels on the *German Ideology* manuscript, Marx had begun to think of 'real life' as centring on the economic realm, the realm that was scorned, bracketed or treated disdainfully by thinkers of a 'philosophical' persuasion and even, indeed, by thinkers of a 'materialist' bent such as Feuerbach. Marx in 1845 was in the course of adopting priorities he was never to abandon, priorities entailing historical analysis, empirical research and the 'critique of political economy'. This critique, Marx was convinced, could galvanize an otherwise inert or cowed proletariat into becoming a class-conscious *Klasse für sich*, 'misery conscious of its misery'. In *The Poverty of Philosophy* Marx castigated those 'who see in misery only misery, without remarking its revolutionary, subversive side which will overthrow the old society'. Marx's critique was in other words to be resolutely practical, an entry into real world politics and 'the language of real life', and as such it was an approach much closer to the ground, much more practical and pragmatic, than the socialist speculation in which Marx had soaked himself in Paris, and much more practical and political than the 'poaching of snipe existing only in the mind' he had encountered among the Germans. Marx's critique was to be his way of setting himself free from the vapid, self-indulgent, moralistic posturing of the self-absorbed German 'ideologists' who had so exasperated him in the early 1840s, and who exasperated him still.

While the political economy that was the object of Marx's critique was not an ideology in the same sense that the posturings of Stirner, Proudhon, the Bauers and Grün were, it was not free from ideological elements in a different and perhaps more insidious sense. It was a body of thought that purported to describe and analyse in a neutral, objective and 'scientific' way, but which could nevertheless be characterized – and was characterized by Marx – as being tendentious, myopic, selective, distorted and partial in the sense that its adumbration is in the interests of the possessing classes. Political economy is demonstrably not ideologically neutral or innocent. It awaits – it needs – the exposure which Marx in one way or another will spend the remainder of his life bringing to bear on it.

It is here that the arguments of *The Holy Family*, *The German Ideology* and *The Poverty of Philosophy* can be seen as continuing the work the *Economic and Philosophic Manuscripts* had initiated. Marx was never to relinquish his insistence – given memorable, startling expression in *The German Ideology* – that the primary or primal historical act of the human species, no matter what the 'ideological reflexes and echoes' of scholars and philosophers might claim, must be the production of material means to satisfy survival needs. Then new needs arise, alongside new means of satisfying them, means which we will sooner or later devise. The dynamism of human needs is in principle infinite, though in practice often constrained. Satisfying our needs entails cooperation, organization, division of labour, industry, commerce, language, consciousness: 'as individuals express their life, so they are'; 'it is not consciousness which determines life, but life which determines consciousness.' Marx and Engels were to repeat this point forcefully in the *Manifesto of the Communist Party*:

> Does it require deep intuition to comprehend that man's ideas, views and conceptions change with every change in the conditions of his material existence, in his social relations, and in his social life? . . . What else does the history of ideas prove, than that intellectual production changes its character in proportion as material production is changed? The ruling ideas of each age have ever been the ideas of its ruling class.[4]

To say this is in no way to deny the specificity of capitalism. It is rather to underscore this specificity. In modern society productive forces do not belong and cannot belong to those who do the work, and this obliges us to look at property relations as well as productive forces, and then to overcome the various forms taken by the division of labour in capitalist society. This division of labour is constraining in an unprecedented manner. Marx and Engels are concerned to stigmatize capitalism's 'all engrossing system of specializing and sorting men, that development in a man of one single faculty at the expense of all the others'. They believed that we must by contrast 'provide each individual with the social latitude he needs to develop his life to the fullest', and there is a great deal of content and amplitude to this conviction. Plato's *Republic* had outlined a division of labour that assigned different tasks to different people on the basis of *people's* differences in aptitude, inclination and talent. Adam Smith had by contrast outlined a division of labour that was in fact a division of *tasks*. Plato's goal had been social and political justice; Smith's, the accumulation of wealth. Labour as a modern economic category no longer has anything to do with the specific characteristics of any particular labourer. Everyone must do the same thing in the same way if as many commodities as possible are to be produced and exchanged. We are now speaking not of labour but of labour *power*, a category that tells us as much about a particular labourer as 'horse power' tells us about a particular horse.

Most extant editions of *The German Ideology* append Marx's 'Theses on Feuerbach', and for good reason – even though the theses are gnomic and aphoristic and were written, presumably, for the sake of Marx's self-clarification. They are theses *on Feuerbach* mainly in the sense that Feuerbach himself inspired them with the following words from his *Vorlesungen über das Wesen der Religion*:

> The negation of the world beyond implies acceptance of this world; the negation of a better life after death implies the demand for a better life on this earth; thus this better life, otherwise a sterile and useless objective, becomes a matter of duty and of conscious human activity. There can be no doubt about the flagrant injustice of some having everything and others having nothing . . . The only conclusion to be drawn from the present injustice and suffering in human existence is the will and effort to change these evils.[5]

Engels discovered and published Marx's 'Theses' only after Marx's death. They were later characterized by Maximilien Rubel as the vade mecum of Marxism. They cover various philosophical staples (materialism, idealism, humanity, nature, society, activity, history, philosophy itself). Feuerbach had supposed that nature gave immediate truth to sense-perception. But nature to Marx – think back to the *Manuscripts* – is a process, not a thing or a state, a process that undergoes transformation by virtue of human action within and upon it. It was idealism, and not the 'old materialism' of the Enlightenment, that had better understood our 'active side'. In so doing it moved beyond the stage or plateau of static episte-mological contemplation, of contemplation seen as registration by the mind of objects outside its ambit. Both mind and matter are in effect involved in 'practical-critical' activity. Making sense of the world is a purposive, constitutive activity that cannot be reduced to mere 'contemplation'. 'The dispute over the reality or non-reality of thinking that is isolated from practice is a purely scholastic question.'

If we simply assert that people are the products or the out-comes of their circumstances, it could follow that they are unfit to found society anew – which is why revolutionary activism does not admit of being grafted onto the 'old materialism' of the French Enlightenment in the first place. Instead, the changing of self and the changing of circumstances must coincide and overlap. The penumbra is revolutionary praxis. This leads us into *The Poverty of Philosophy* as well as *The German Ideology*, and indeed into the *Manifesto of the Communist Party* into the bargain. 'Communism', says *The German Ideology*, 'is for us not . . . an ideal to which reality will have to adjust itself. We call communism the real movement which abolishes the present state of affairs.' The *Manifesto* follows suit:

> the theoretical problems of the communists are in no way based
> on ideas or principles that have been invented, or discovered,
> by this or that would-be universal reformer. They merely express,
> in general terms, actual relations, springing from an existing

class struggle, from an historical movement going on under our very eyes.[6]

We shall revert to the *Manifesto* after touching on *The Poverty of Philosophy*. Marx had first met Pierre-Joseph Proudhon (1809–1865) only in September 1844, while he was working on *The Holy Family*. 'In the course of long discussions, which sometimes went on all through the night,' Marx later disclosed, 'I infected him, to his great detriment, with a Hegelianism he could not go deeply into because he did not know German.' The tutelary tone of Marx's recollection is deliberately deceptive. In 1844 Proudhon was a celebrated theoretician in France with four well-known books – books certainly known to Marx – to his name. That Marx by comparison was an unknown did nothing to stop him from attempting to undermine Proudhon's reputation once and for all, three years later and quite unsuccessfully, in *The Poverty of Philosophy*. Earlier, however, Marx had mentioned Proudhon's writings in passing in the *Economic and Philosophic Manuscripts*, and had even, after a fashion, defended Proudhon (in *The Holy Family*) against Edgar Bauer's misrepresentations of his beliefs. Even so, the criticisms Marx levelled so unrelentingly in *The Poverty of Philosophy* were not lacking in precedent (or in subsequent amplification). The only pages of Marx's *Economic and Philosophic Manuscripts* to find any kind of way into print during his lifetime were those almost copied verbatim into *The Holy Family*, some of them to the effect that Proudhon as an economist fails to appreciate that wages 'are only a necessary consequence of the alienation of labour'. Thus 'an enforced increase in wages', as advocated by Proudhon,

> would be nothing more than a better remuneration of slaves and would not restore, either to the worker or the work, their human significance or worth . . . Even the equality of wages,

Pierre-Joseph Proudhon, in a portrait by fellow anarchist Gustave Courbet.

which Proudhon demands, would only change the relation of the present-day worker to his work into the relation of all men to work. Society would then be conceived as an abstract capitalist.[7]

On the other hand, as *The Holy Family* goes on to indicate, Proudhon's understanding in his first *Mémoire* of private property as private property relations that are connected with the growth of wage labour is to be commended over the political economists' objectivistic and determinist laws, which by comparison overlook the human aspect of economic relations. In a letter to J. B. von Schweitzer Marx commends Proudhon's 'provocative defiance, laying hands on the economic "holy of holies"', private property, adding, however, the rider that Proudhon's 'criticism of political economy is still bound by the premises of political economy'. Proudhon in the upshot 'abolishes political-economic estrangement within political-economic estrangement',[8] an accusation Marx levels in both *The Holy Family* and *The Poverty of Philosophy* (and had also issued *en passant* in *The German Ideology*).

The Poverty of Philosophy, because it plays down Proudhon's anti-communism but excoriates his economics and dialectics, has come down to us mainly as a concise prefiguration of Marxian economics, in fact as the only book on economics Marx saw into print before 1859. Even the polemic with which it is leavened can serve to remind us that politics is never absent from Marx's economic analyses.

> Proletariat and wealth are antinomies; as such they form a single whole. They are both forms of the word 'private property' (*Privateigenthum*) . . . The proletariat . . . is compelled as proletariat to abolish itself and thereby its opposite, the conditions for its existence, what makes it the proletariat, i.e. private property . . . It cannot free itself without abolishing the conditions of its own life [as proletariat] . . . the proletariat can and must

emancipate itself. But it cannot emancipate itself without transcending the conditions of its own life. It cannot transcend the conditions of its own life without transcending all the inhuman conditions of present-day society which are summed up in its own situation . . . It is not a question of what this or that proletarian or even the whole proletariat imagines to be its aim. It is a question of what the proletariat is and what it consequently is compelled to do.[9]

But what Marx adds to these imperatives in *The Poverty of Philosophy* is of vital importance: he distinguishes a class in itself (*Klasse an sich*) from a class for itself (*Klasse für sich*). The former is defined by its social placement vis-à-vis other classes; the latter, instead of resting content with being defined from without in this way, sets about defining itself consciously and actively. This is a distinction to which we will return when we turn to *The Eighteenth Brumaire of Louis Bonaparte*; but it is also a distinction Marx puts to work in the pages of *The Poverty of Philosophy*, a distinction between awareness and consciousness. It is on the cusp of this distinction that theory and the theorist enter in. Marx's words are ambitious indeed:

Just as the economists are the scientific representatives of the bourgeois class, so the socialists and communists are the theoreticians of the proletarian class. So long as the proletariat is not yet sufficiently developed to constitute itself as a class, and consequently so long as the struggle of the proletariat with the bourgeoisie has not yet assumed a political character, and the productive forces are not yet sufficiently developed in the bosom of the bourgeoisie to enable us to catch a glimpse of the material conditions necessary for the emancipation of the proletariat and the formation of a new society, these theoreticians are merely utopians who, to meet the wants of the oppressed classes, improvise systems and go in search of a regenerative science. But in the measure that history moves forward, and with it the struggle of the proletariat assumes clearer outlines, they no longer need to seek science in their minds; they have only to take note of what is happening before their eyes and become its mouthpiece. So long as they look for science and merely make systems, so long as they are at the beginning of the struggle, they see in poverty nothing but poverty, without seeing in it the subversive, revolutionary side, which will overthrow the old society. From this moment science, which is the product of the historical movement, has associated itself consciously with it, has ceased to be doctrinaire and has become revolutionary.[10]

The Manifesto of the Communist Party

At the beginning of 1846 Marx and Engels established in Brussels a Communist Corresponding Committee which would, in Marx's words, provide

> both a discussion of scientific questions and a critical appraisal of popular writings and socialist propaganda that can be conducted in Germany by these means. But the main aim . . . will be to put German socialists in touch with English and French socialists, to keep foreigners informed of the socialist movements that will develop in Germany and to inform the Germans in Germany of the progress of socialism in France and England. In this way differences of opinion will be brought to light and we shall obtain an exchange of ideas and impartial opinion.

In the event, overtures to or contacts with the French may have been stymied by Marx's 1847 attack on Proudhon, *La Misère de la philosophie*, an attack he took care to write in French and have published in Paris. We have already remarked that as an attempt to discredit Proudhon, Marx's principled, but tactless and ill-timed, book failed: after its appearance, as before it, Proudhon was by far the better known of the two theorists, at least inside France. Marx in 1846–7 had rather better luck (or judgement) with communists in London, to whom he made overtures, suggesting that they form a Corresponding Committee that would work with the one in Brussels. This suggestion appears to have been taken up and acted upon. Marx was duly invited to join the London-based League of the Just, and did so, attending a congress in London in June 1847 that brought together the London sections of the League with the Brussels Corresponding Committee. It was at the London congress that the Communist League was born; it was at the League's second congress, also held in London in November to December 1847, that Marx and Engels were commissioned to prepare a statement of the League's aims, a statement which within months took shape in published form as the *Manifesto of the Communist Party.*

One would be hard put to deduce these comparatively small and rather conspiratorial beginnings from the tone of the *Manifesto* itself, which is brisk, brash, confident, world-changing and not conspiratorial at all. The *Manifesto* reads as though it could sweep everything before it. It reads this way because it was designed to read this way: as a document ambitious enough to bring about the conditions of its own successful implementation. But influence and reputation in the long term is one thing, immediate significance at the time of first publication something else again. The *Manifesto* first saw the light of day soon after the Paris uprising of February 1848; it had no causal effect on the February days. Thereafter it was one of many revolutionary clarion calls that were sounded throughout the rest of the would-be *annus mirabilis*. Nevertheless the *Manifesto* was more vividly written and historically informed than the others, its verbal power should not be mistaken for influence on the events (or non-events) of 1848 – that historical turning point, as A.J.P. Taylor so memorably called it, when history signally failed to turn. 'The Communists', said the *Manifesto*, 'turn their attention chiefly to Germany', but the effects the document may have had there in 1848 are not easily disentangled from those of the physical presence of Marx in Cologne, or from the effects of a pamphlet of March 1848, 'The Demands of the Communist Party in Germany', an adaptation of the transitional programme of the *Manifesto* to conditions in Germany. The complication here stems from the fact that that this later pamphlet has nothing specifically 'communist' about it, since the need in Germany continued to be what it had been for some time: the destruction of absolutism on the part of all groups opposed to it. Even so, it is clear from the *Manifesto* itself as well as from all other subsequent writings –

The cover of the *Communist Manifesto*, published in London in February 1848.

A contemporary lithograph of the 1848 Revolution in Berlin, part of a Europe-wide wave of insurrections.

Marx was to write nothing that was incompatible with the *Manifesto* and the *Manifesto*'s prescriptions – that Marx's own thought had hardened. That it now had an edge to it that most 'socialists' as opposed to 'communists' lacked was noticed at the time. Friedrich Lessner, a Hamburg worker, recalled Marx at the second congress (1846) of the Communist League:

> His speech was brief, convincing and compelling in its logic. He never said a superfluous word; every sentence was a thought, and every thought a necessary link in the chain of his demonstration. Marx had nothing of the dreamer about him. The more I realized the difference between the communism of Weiltling's time and that of the *Communist Manifesto*, the more clearly I saw that Marx represented the manhood of socialist thought.

It is noteworthy that Marx for his part never described himself as a socialist prior to the Paris Commune of 1871, always instead as a communist. There are good reasons for Marx's insistence on this, reasons having nothing at all to do with the twentieth-century history of what came to be called communism. Socialism long pre-dated Marx; it was already flourishing on French soil when Marx arrived in Paris in 1843, as a congeries of movements which earnestly but in varying proportions advocated economic amelioration and legislative protection for the workers, universal suffrage, civil rights of association and freedom of opinion, co-operative institutions, and cultural opportunities for the poor. The utopian socialists of the 1830s had had a great deal to say about the workers, but not much to say *to* them. Communism, too, was flourishing in Paris at the time, but it was flourishing separately from socialism; what was distinctive about communism can be seen in its drastic points of difference from the thought of one prominent thinker who delighted in the appellation 'socialist', Louis Blanc, who did not believe either in the organization of the revolutionary working class or in the abolition of private property relations. Communists, by contrast, espoused both beliefs with some virulence, and rejected the socialists' often positive attitude towards the state (an attitude admittedly not shared by Proudhon, Fourier or Owen); the communists' lineage may be traced back to the *cercle social* of the French Revolution – Leclerc, Roux, Babeuf and Buonarroti – whose writings were among those that Marx had studied in Paris.

It is frequently forgotten today that communism made its bid only after the socialist movement had become organized, conscious, active, doctrinaire and French; this helps explain the otherwise puzzling inclusion of 'French Radicals' among the rogues' gallery of anti-communists listed in the *Manifesto*'s second sentence. Lorenz von Stein's *Der Sozialismus und Kommunismus des heutigen Frankreichs* (1842) had designated as 'socialists' the three writers Marx in the *Manifesto* was for his part to consider 'critical-utopian' ideologues: Saint-Simon, Fourier and Owen. Marx was to dismiss these and their followers as fanatical sectarians building castles in the air. Indeed, Marx in the 1840s came to believe that socialism, like Proudhonism, was by definition utopian and doctrinaire, and that it was by the same token a false friend to communism. He thought that for this reason its very name should be avoided. Moreover, not only were socialists utopian, or reformist, or both; they were also invariably members of eminently middle-class movements craving respectability, as opposed to the communists who (whether utopians or not) were at least autonomous and (predominantly) proletarian.

Socialism by the 1840s had not become – and in the eyes of Marx could never become – the common creed of the working class, whereas the communism of Etienne Cabet or Wilhelm Weitling had the considerable merit of endorsing class war, revolution and the abolition of private property relations, even if these did propound their beliefs in a rough-hewn way. Marx, whose personal intolerance was notorious, tended to adhere to revolutionaries who were on the correct side of the communist-socialist hiatus; he greatly admired Weitling and broke with him most reluctantly, even though Weitling tended to recruit among skilled artisans rather than the nascent proletariat and refused at times even to recognize the role of an organized working-class movement. 'The theory of the communists', said the *Manifesto* (which proclaims in its first sentence Marx and Engels's adherence to communism rather than their invention of it), 'may be summed up in a single sentence: the abolition of private property (*Aufhebung des Privat-Eigenthums*)'[11] – a sentence that was designed explicitly to distinguish the authors' adopted communism from the *Güter-gemeinschaft* or *communauté des biens* so earnestly preached by the socialists. In accordance with this, Marx was baldly to write, some 25 years later, that the (First) International 'ha[d] been founded to replace socialist or semi-socialist sects with the real organization of the working class'.

The distinction between socialism and communism that Marx outlined in the *Manifesto* was maintained in the meantime throughout Marx's more detailed historical writings. In *The Class Struggles in France* and *The Eighteenth Brumaire of Louis Bonaparte*, the basic distinction that the *Manifesto* had outlined is maintained: the 'socialist doctrinaires' (Ledru-Rollin, Lamartine, Blanc) are always distinguished from and compared unfavourably with 'the proletariat's real revolutionaries' (Blanqui, Cabet, Raspail). Marx felt very strongly about the distinction between those who could be curtly dismissed as 'socialist miracle workers' on the one hand, and those with whom he had identified himself and cast his lot on the other. After all, the whole point of the *Manifesto* and, later, the International, was to eschew conspiratorialism and to present to the world, openly and brazenly, the views and aims of a movement. This movement, though numerically weak, was an authentic, autonomous, working-class, international movement dedicated to a type of revolutionary programme that had transcended the elitism of Blanqui as well as the conspiratorialism of Babeuf, together with reformism of any stripe.

The *Manifesto*'s opening line – '*Ein Gespenst geht um in Europa*' – was first rendered into English by Helen Macfarlane in 1848 as 'A frightful hobgoblin stalks throughout Europe.' While this was an egregious mistranslation, it had – despite itself – the merit of invoking the horror stories of Andersen and the Brothers Grimm, which were abroad during the 1840s as children's books or fairy tales, and thus of suggesting that those who took this 'hobgoblin' seriously should simply grow up. Macfarlane may in this sense have been less carried away than Jacques Derrida in his more recent book, *Spectres of Marx*.[12] The spectre said to be 'haunting' Europe in the *Manifesto* is not, *pace* Derrida, what the French call a *revenant* or ghost, coming from beyond the grave to torment the living. 'Haunts' or 'is haunting' is if anything a rather more strained translation than is 'stalks' of *umgeht . . . in*, *umgehen* being a fairly anodyne verb of motion; if I say of some location that it is 'one of my old haunts', I mean that I used to go there, not that I am now dead.

Who, then, has anything to fear from Marx's spectre? Marx himself nominates a holy alliance, a choice of words that suggests the real-life Holy Alliance of the 'Congress System' – 'of Pope and Tsar, Metternich and Guizot, French Radicals and German police'; these – the anti-Communist party – have invented or conjured up the spectre in question, and are now bent upon seeing to it that the rest of us quake in our boots at its onset. Marx for his part is unafraid, indeed welcoming, of the spectre the Holy Alliance and its minions had invoked in what Terrell Carver's translation of the *Manifesto* has as their 'witch-hunt' – even though or precisely because witch-hunts always find what they are looking for, to the extent of invoking or conjuring it up out of thin air. (As Louis Brandeis once put it, 'men feared witches and burnt women'.) Marx's aim was to dispel such fears. 'It is high time that the Communists lay before the world their perspectives, their goals, their principles, and counterpose to the horror stories [or 'fairy tales'] of communism a manifesto of the party itself.'[13] If the spectre stalking the land is spirit not made flesh, this means spirit not *yet* made flesh – unsubstantiated, perhaps, but awaiting the substantiation that Marx and his readers can give it.

Marx's spectre, that is to say, points forward, projectively and prospectively, not (as Derrida's ghost stories would have it) backwards and retroactively. There is nothing dreadful or *unheimlich* about it except to those who have prior cause to dread its advent. To the rest of us it is a tocsin, a call to action. Again, a pattern emerges, and it is in no obvious sense what is usually considered a 'materialist' one. Malcolm Bull calls attention to beliefs that are 'everywhere condemned but nowhere to be found'. Fervent denunciations of the evils of atheism, for instance, pre-dated, preceded and (in a sense) provoked the appearance of real, self-professed, flesh-and-blood atheists on the historical stage.

These duly manifested themselves only after their adversaries had prepared the way for their advent. Again, 'just as the invention of atheism had taken place without anybody actually advocating this position', so too

> the invention and repudiation of anarchism occurred without the intervention of any anarchists. No-one espoused an explicitly anarchist position until William Godwin, and no-one used 'anarchist' in a positive sense until Proudhon. However, that did not stop 'anarchists' from being roundly abused

prior to their appearance. Later in the nineteenth century, 'there was no-one claiming to be a nihilist, just a chorus of . . . moralists arguing that nihilism was an outrage'. Atheism, anarchism, nihilism: these constitute what Bull calls a 'series of spectral negations', each of which 'is not so much unrealizable as temporarily disembodied'.[14] Those who came to embody such positions were confident that they could act out positively a role that others were bent upon condemning out of hand as being unconscionable.

Marx when he wrote the *Manifesto* was confident in this very sense. Why else would he have insisted that we are 'compelled to face with sober senses' something seen by others as an instance of sheer delirium or nightmare? The disembodiment of Marx's spectre is purely provisional. It awaits the embodiment that the *Manifesto* (with no small flourish) duly proceeded to give it. Marx in its pages is openly, publicly, ostentatiously, brazenly pinning down communism, giving it the form, substance and clear agenda it had lacked. Marx was giving voice to something altogether original, seizing the time, giving form and substance to something that might appear threatening as mere form to the craven and the cowed. Marx's *Manifesto*, an instance of theoretical audacity, changed the rules of the game once and for all.

The dimensions of what Marx accomplished cannot be gauged or appreciated if we isolate the *Manifesto* and make it a set piece or a *pièce d'occasion*. To reduce or consign it to the conditions of its inception would be doubly misleading, since the document circulated widely and became well known only when it was republished in the 1870s. The *Manifesto* straddled or transcended the circumstances of its inception. The *Manifesto*'s premonitory character is such that the agenda that leaps from its pages would extend the scope and scale of politics and of theory further than these boundaries had ever stretched before. At the present day, the Marxist ideal of 'the revolutionary unity of theory and practice' has frequently and justly been reviled for its various attempted justifications of the reprehensible. What is often forgotten is that at the moment of its inception it was a Marxian ideal, not a Marxist one. It had yet to become a mere catchword or slogan or empty phrase. Its promise had yet to be betrayed. It is thus worth the effort of trying to recapture what it entailed at its birth.

To set about doing so is to be confronted with a surprise, as Marshall Berman has pointed out. The surprise takes the form of a disarming admission: 'The bourgeoisie has played a highly revolutionary part in history.' Has Marx come not to bury the bourgeoisie but to praise it? – to praise it, indeed, in more exorbitant terms than even some of its straightforward apologists had managed to muster up? The bourgeoisie, uniquely, had in Marx's words 'demonstrated what human activity can accomplish. It has executed marvels quite different from Egyptian pyramids, Roman aqueducts and Gothic cathedrals; it has carried out expeditions quite different from barbarian invasions and crusades.'[15] Marx emphasizes the bourgeoisie's genius for activity expressed in great projects of physical construction: mills, factories, roads, bridges, canals, railways – the pyramids, aqueducts and cathedrals of the modern age, if you will. Nor is this all. There are also immense movements of peoples, populations – to cities, to frontiers, to new lands, to new continents. These are migrations the bourgeoisie has sometimes inspired, sometimes brutally enforced, sometimes subsidized and always exploited for profit.

Throughout, it is the activity of the bourgeoisie that Marx celebrates and dramatizes; he is not primarily interested in the things, the material objects and artefacts, the bourgeoisie creates and utilizes. Remarkable though these are, they are but signs, traces, residues. Marx's emphasis is on the processes, powers and energies these material objects represent: people working, moving, cultivating, communicating, organizing and reorganizing external nature and, with it, themselves, in endlessly renewed circuits of activity. Marx does not dwell on inventions or technological 'innovations'. These are effects, not causes, epiphenomena of the processes and of the energies the processes involve, energies which charge and re-charge successive human projects.

The bourgeoisie is however obliged to close itself off from its own possibilities, possibilities that are the richest that human history has ever put on offer. 'In scarcely one hundred years of class rule the bourgeoisie has created more massive, and more colossal forces of production than have all preceding generations put together.' Yet there is a sense in which the bourgeoisie cannot reap the benefit. The realization of the possibilities the bourgeoisie has opened up awaits those who are to break its power. While the bourgeoisie has opened up all manner of activities at which we may justly marvel, the only activity that matters to the bourgeoisie itself is the prosaic one of making money and accumulating capital. All bourgeois enterprises, whatever their form or scope may be, are but means to the end of accumulation. The bourgeoisie cannot reap what its members sow; all their manifold accomplishments are but means to an anterior end. The powers, processes and energies that Marx celebrates are but incidental by-products, of passing, transitory interest to those bourgeois who bring them into being and keep them in existence.

Even so, the bourgeoisie has done what no other ruling class in history had ever done before them: 'it creates a world in its own image'.[16] It has proved what organized, concerted human action – what man considered as *homo faber* – can do. But it must shrink from the implications of its own achievement. Others are freer to look down the vistas the bourgeoisie has opened up than are members of the bourgeoisie themselves. It is others who can afford to ask questions the bourgeoisie would regard as badly put: why should human activity be limited or even geared to profit? By extension, why should those who can see what concerted activity can do proceed supinely to accept the given structure of bourgeois rule? After all, the world is changeable, labile, open. It has been changed, dramatically, suddenly and out of all recognition, within the living memory of many people. Why then should it not be changed again, this time more thoroughly? If the bourgeoisie has shown us, unintentionally, what organized, concerted human activity is capable of accomplishing, why should those who can learn from the bourgeois example not accomplish yet more? And why should this not be done, this time around, more decisively, more intentionally, more purposefully, more freely?

It is perhaps the virtues for which the Shakespeare-loving Marx praises the bourgeoisie that will bury it in the end. If the bourgeoisie 'cannot exist without constantly revolutionizing the means of production', it has made explicit a capacity for what might at first glance seem contradictory: permanent change. The bourgeois epoch is characterized by perpetual upheaval and renewal in the sense that the individual bourgeois is obliged to innovate constantly, simply in order to keep his head above water. To fail to effect changes constantly is to become the victim of changes effected by others who are less reticent. This means that the revolutionizing of production spills over into every area of life in such a way that dynamism, movement and flux permeate everything.

The bourgeoisie cannot exist without continually revolutionizing the instruments of production, hence the relations of production, and therefore social relations as a whole. By contrast, the first condition of existence of all earlier manufacturing classes was the unaltered maintenance of the old mode of production. The continual transformation of production, the uninterrupted convulsion of all social conditions, a perpetual uncertainty and motion distinguish the epoch of the bourgeoisie from all earlier ones. All the settled, age-old relations with their train of time-honoured preconceptions and viewpoints are dissolved; all newly-formed ones become outmoded before they can ossify. Everything fixed and feudal goes up in smoke, everything sacred is profaned, and [people] are forced to take a down-to-earth view of their circumstances, their multifarious relationships.[17]

Evidently, there is more to this picture than just mutability or volatility. There is derangement of the senses, for one thing. 'Uninterrupted convulsion' and 'perpetual uncertainty' are giddy, vertiginous categories that would destabilize or subvert most known societies. But they serve to strengthen and characterize bourgeois society. Marx is characterizing a kind of *mise en abyme*: stability – that which sustains most known or most imagined societies – is here not a promise but a threat, akin to slow death or entropy. This extraordinary state of affairs – capitalist society appearing to destabilize stability itself, the most basic prerequisite of any conceivable society – has to it an obverse and a converse. Its obverse is nostalgia for an idealized pre-capitalist state of affairs, a reflex from which Marx wished to steer his readers once and for all. (Revolutionists must learn not to yearn for 'settled, age-old relations' venerated by nothing but time.) Its converse is the acceptance of the very renewal and mobility on which revolutionists could thrive – capitalism having imposed this openness to change upon people anyway. Faced with it, we have only to ask: in a system where all human accomplishments and relationships are suddenly and newly volatile, how can it be that capitalist forms and capitalist forms alone can endure and hold steady? To ask this question is to raise the possibility, already raised in the privacy of Marx's 1844 *Manuscripts*, of self-development, freed from the demands and distortions of the market, and to see that the possibility of such freedom is both raised in and denied by capitalism.

The *Manifesto of the Communist Party* moves beyond *The German Ideology* when it identifies 'law, morality, religion' as being to the communist 'so many bourgeois prejudices, behind which lurk in ambush just as many bourgeois interests'.[18] *The German Ideology* had proffered a view of ideology as 'speculative idealism', the German ideologists having believed that consciousness is an autonomous realm that admits of being studied and explained in its own terms, independently of social relations. Marx in *The German Ideology* had held that ideology as speculative idealism inverts the relationship between the human subject and the world in presenting the latter in a topsy-turvy manner: 'in ideology men and their circumstances appear upside down as in a camera obscura'.[19] Ideology here means idealism rather than apology, but in Marx's later works bias and apology become defining features of ideology. In the political writings (*The Class Struggles in France*, *The Eighteenth Brumaire of Louis Bonaparte* and *The Civil War in France*) the 'ideological representatives of the bourgeoisie' are straightforward apologists for bourgeois interests. The economic writings (the *Grundrisse*, *Capital* and *Theories of Surplus Value*) tend on the other hand to distinguish between such open, unashamed advocacy and the work of honest, disinterested investigators who might unintentionally idealize, justify or absolutize something. These latter universalize their points of view or forms of thought not because it is in their interest to do so but because they find them 'natural' or self-evident. Bias need not be intentional or self-interested, but if the bias is ideological it will be slanted towards, and will thus defend, legitimize or speak for, one group or class rather than another or others.

This does not mean that ideology is the same as justification. Marx justified capitalism in the *Manifesto*, in that he was prepared to admit its positive features, but he was not an apologist for capitalism in the way that the 'political economists' (Adam Smith, David Ricardo and others) were. Nor is ideology defined simply by falsity or mendaciousness. An idea may be false without being ideological, and illusions have no necessary ideological function. Ideologies are rather always appropriate to those who proffer them, whether or not those persons do so with the intent to deceive or mislead. Nor again are ideologies necessarily imposed on people; they may be accepted by people, quite freely – as perhaps in the famous early characterization of religion as 'the opium of the people'. Opium, after all, is taken, and not as a rule administered. Ideologies must be intelligible and appear to 'make sense' to those who accept them as well as to those who disseminate them. But to the extent that ideologies are not instances of 'speculative idealism' but systematically biased bodies of thought favouring some group or class over another or others, their mere intellectual inversion (as in *The German Ideology*'s metaphor of the camera obscura) will not suffice to dislodge their hold.

4

London, 1849–83

Little thinking that it would be his home for the rest of his life, Marx arrived in London in August 1849 having been summarily expelled yet again from France – a France that had so recently invited and welcomed him back after the February revolution in 1848, the 'beautiful revolution' he anatomized in *The Class Struggles in France*, but a France that had since the February days endured the *coup d'état* engineered by the preposterous Louis-Napoléon (a coup which Marx was to anatomize in *The Eighteenth Brumaire of Louis Bonaparte*). Space forbids any adequate account of Marx's activities during the would-be *annus mirabilis* that stretched between and beyond these events; suffice it to say that they were busy and complex enough to merit another book in their own right, involving as they did agitation, propaganda, travel to and from France, Belgium, Germany and Austria, arrests, imprisonment and trials at which Marx's eloquence in his own defence helped get him acquitted. What went into this forcefulness and eloquence was to be recalled by Pavel Annenkov:

> Marx . . . was the type of man who is made up of energy, will and unshakeable conviction. He was most remarkable in his appearance. He had a shock of deep black hair and hairy hands and his coat was buttoned wrong; but he looked like a man with the right and power to demand respect, no matter how he appeared before you and no matter what he did. His movements were

clumsy but confident and self-reliant, his ways defied the usual
conventions in human relations, but they were dignified and
somewhat disdainful; his sharp metallic voice was wonderfully
adapted to the radical judgments that he passed on persons and
things. He always spoke in imperative words that would brook no
contradiction and were made all the sharper by the almost pain-
ful impression of the tone which ran through every thing he said.[1]

Wilhelm Liebknecht has left us a more detailed physical (indeed,
well nigh anatomical) picture of Marx in the 1850s, when Liebknecht
first knew him. 'He was in fact very powerful. His height was above
the average, his shoulders broad, his chest well-developed and
his legs well-proportioned, although the spine was a little long
in comparison with the length of his legs, a tendency often to be
found amongst the Jews.'[2] (Indeed.) Liebknecht was not alone in
noticing that Marx, like Goethe, gave the impression while sitting
of being taller standing than he really was. His overall reminiscences
of his friend were salutary in the extreme:

> no-one could be kinder or fairer than Marx in giving others
> their due. He was too great to be envious, jealous or vain. But
> he had as deadly a hatred for the false greatness and pretended
> fame of swaggering incapacity and vulgarity as for any kind
> of deceit and pretence . . . He never struck an attitude, he was
> always himself . . . As long as social or political grounds did
> not make it undesirable, he always spoke his mind completely
> and without any reserve . . . Marx was never a hypocrite. He
> was absolutely incapable of it, just like an unsophisticated child.
> His wife often called him 'my big baby', and nobody, not even
> Engels, knew or understood him better than she did.

The Marx family's domestic circumstances in the course of what
Nicholaevsky and Maenchen-Helfen call their 'sleepless night of

Karl and Jenny Marx.

exile' in London, prolonged as this exile turned out to be, were grim in the extreme. The Marxes had seven children – Jenny Caroline (1844–1883); Jenny Laura (1845–1911); Edgar, also known as Musch or Mouche (1847–1855); Henry Edward Guy, also known as Guido or Foxchen (1849–1850); Jenny Eveline Frances, known as Franziska (1851–1852); Eleanor, known as Tussy (1855–1898); and one stillborn baby, who died in 1857 even before being named.

The very dates are, as the French say, *à faire trembler*; the Marxes stumbled from one tragedy to the next. ('*Beatus ille der keine Familie hat*' – 'Fortunate is he who has no family', as Marx put it in 1854 in the privacy of a letter to Engels.) By the time that Eleanor, the youngest surviving daughter was born, in Soho, Henry Edward Guy and Jenny Eveline Frances had died, in 1850 and 1852 respectively. Edgar was to die later in the year of Eleanor's birth. Of the other two surviving children, Jenny had been born in 1844 in Paris, Laura in 1845 in Brussels. At first, in the period of retrenchment that came in the wake of the failure of the 1848 revolutionary wave, the family's poverty – 'blazing carbuncles and mounting debts' was how Marx summed it all up – was dire. ('Whatever happens', said Marx in 1867, 'the bourgeoisie will remember my carbuncles.') In the words of a surprisingly observant and literate Prussian spy, in 1852:

Marx lives in one of the worst, therefore one of the cheapest, quarters of London [Soho] . . . In the whole apartment there is not one clean and solid piece of furniture. Everything is broken, tattered and torn, with half an inch of dust over everything and the greatest disorder everywhere . . . In the middle of the salon there is a large old-fashioned table covered with an oil-cloth, and on it there lie manuscripts, books, newspapers, as well as the children's toys, the rags and tatters of his wife's sewing basket, several cups with broken rims, knives, forks, lamps, an inkpot, tumblers, Dutch clay pipes, tobacco, ash – in a word, everything topsy-turvy, and all on the same table. A seller of second hand goods would be ashamed to give away such a remarkable collection of odds and ends.

When you enter Marx's room smoke and tobacco fumes make your eyes water so much that for a moment you seem to be groping about in a cavern, but gradually, as you grow accustomed to the fog, you can make out certain objects which distinguish themselves from the surrounding haze. [Marx – as an aside – was famously to observe some fifteen years later that *Capital* would not pay for the cigars he smoked while writing it]. Everything is dirty, and covered with dust, so that to sit down becomes a thoroughly dangerous business . . . if you sit down, you risk a pair of trousers . . .[3]

In general, as Eleanor's biographer Yvone Kapp puts it, 'the laughing, loving parents of Eleanor's childhood were racked by the most sordid misery and distress . . . Karl Marx was bought to the point of desperation and Jenny Marx to the verge of a nervous breakdown.'[4] Kapp is not exaggerating. The Marxes lived at 28 Dean St, Soho – an address at which three of their then six children died – for six dismal, penurious years, being enabled to move to 9 (now 46) Grafton Terrace, Kentish Town, in September 1856, thanks to three bequests to the elder Jenny. They remained at

The Marx family's first London home (1850–56) comprised furnished rooms on the top floor of this house in Dean Street, Soho.

Grafton Terrace for seven and a half years, and were in Jenny Marx's words 'permanently hard up' throughout. In April 1852 Marx had to borrow money to bury his daughter Franziska; in October the same year he pawned his overcoat (not for the first time) in order to buy paper. In the words of Jerrold Siegel:

> Evicted and persecuted, perpetually short of money, hounded by creditors, plagued by illness, attacked and defamed (not always falsely) by former comrades, shattered by the death of their children, the Marx family would experience what [the older] Jenny would later call 'years of great hardship, continual acute privations . . . and real misery'.[5]

On the one hand, in 1857, Engels managed to scrape together £5 a month for the Marx family, a sum he later managed to augment; on the other hand, the *New York Daily Tribune* unilaterally halved Marx's income from journalism the same year. 'Never, I think, was money written about under such a shortage of it', said Marx during the unusually cold winter of 1858, adding wryly that most authors on this particular subject were, by comparison, 'profoundly at peace with the subject of their researches'.[6]

That the family was living from hand to mouth could hardly have been concealed from the daughters. Even so, their later memories of family life were memories suffused with (emotional if not physical) warmth, joy and laughter. Liebknecht, who lived as an exile in London from 1848 to 1862, fondly recalled the Marx family's Sunday outings to Hampstead Heath as a counterweight to 'emigration misery'. The 90-minute walk to Hampstead would start at eleven in the morning. The picnic was substantial: 'a joint of roast veal was the main course, consecrated by tradition', along with 'tea and sugar and occasionally some fruit'. Food was followed either by quiet activities like talk, newspaper reading or rest, or more vigorous ones such as races, sports or donkey rides. The walk

The Marx family, and Engels, on London's Hampstead Heath, a favoured leisure spot.

home was accompanied by songs and stories. So happy were these Sundays that everyone who participated in them looked forward to them all week long, and Liebknecht declared that 'were I to live to a thousand I should never forget them'.[7] The eldest daughter Jenny, who later in life was to be exiled with her husband, Charles Longuet, and their children in Argenteuil (a town that appealed to the French Impressionists and Parisian bourgeois weekenders rather more than it appealed to her), was perhaps never wholly reconciled to the loss of the warm family life she had experienced throughout her youth. But it was Marx's favourite daughter, Eleanor, who recalled it most adoringly:

To those who knew Karl Marx no legend is funnier than the common one which pictures him as a morose, bitter, unbending, unapproachable man, a sort of Jupiter Totans, ever hurling thunder, never known to smile, sitting aloof and alone on Olympus. This picture of the cheeriest, gayest soul that ever breathed, of a man brimming over with humour and good-humour, whose hearty laugh was infectious and irresistible, of the kindest, gentlest, most sympathetic of companions, is a standing wonder – and amusement – to those who know him. In his home life, as in his acquaintances with friends . . . I think one might say that Karl Marx's main characteristics were his unbounded good-humour and his unlimited sympathy . . . A less sweet-tempered man would often have been driven frantic by the constant interruptions, the continual demands made upon him by all sorts of people . . .

To those who are students of human nature, it will not seem strange that this man, who was such a fighter, should at the same time be the kindest and the gentlest of men. They will understand that he could hate so fiercely because he could love so profoundly; that if his trenchant pen could imprison a soul in hell as Dante himself it was because he was so true and tender; that if his sarcastic humour could bite like a corrosive acid, that same humour could be as balm to those in trouble and afflicted . . . Of the many wonderful tales [my father] told me, the most wonderful, the most delightful one was called "Hans Röckle". It went on for months and months; it was a whole series of stories . . . Hans Röckle himself was a Hoffmann-like magician who kept a toyshop and who was always 'hard up.' His shop was full of the most wonderful things – of wooden men and women, giants and dwarfs, kings and queens, workmen and masters, animals and birds, as numerous as Noah got into the ark, tables and chairs, carriages, boxes of all sorts and sizes. And though he was a magician, Hans could never meet his obligations, either to the devil or to the butcher, and was therefore – much against the grain – constantly obliged to sell his toys to the devil. These then went through wonderful adventures – always ending in a return to Hans Röckle's shop . . .[8]

But if – as all surviving memoirs suggest – warmth and good humour permeated and animated the Marxes' family life, these good feelings cannot have altogether displaced or obviated the want and deprivation that continued to punctuate it. In some respects, indeed, the household's *démenagement* in 1856 to the suburbs of Kentish Town made matters worse, not better. Grafton Terrace stood alone at the far reaches of London's northward expansion. Its precincts were (as they say) 'undeveloped', which is to say the roads were as yet unpaved and, London being London, stayed muddy whenever it rained. 'It was a long time', wrote Frau Jenny,

> before I could get used to the complete solitude. I often missed the long walks I had been in the habit of making in the crowded West End streets, the meetings, the clubs, and our favourite public house and homely conversations which had so often helped me to forget the worries of life for a time.

There were now no neighbours to turn to for support when things went wrong, as there had been in Soho. And, the Marxes being the Marxes, things did continue to go wrong. In Jenny Marx's words, again:

> The road to 'respectability' lay open with our ownership of a house. *La vie de bohème* came to an end, and where previously we had fought the battle of poverty in exile freely and openly, now we had the appearance of respectability, and held up our heads again . . . I first came to know the real oppression of exile during this first phase of our truly bourgeois life as Philistines

... Everything conspired to bring about a bourgeois existence, and to enmesh us in it. We could no longer live like bohemians when everyone was a Philistine.[9]

It is not that the family misfortunes now assumed a pattern – there was nothing unrelenting or regularized about them. Rather, they came to adopt a characteristic form. Take a single, pointed example. In Kapp's words, on Christmas Day 1859, 'with everyone ailing in one way or another, [the Marx family] gathered round the imaginary *Weinachtsbaum* to drink the champagne Engels had sent'.[10] This suggests what other surviving evidence also brings to mind: that the Marxes became adept at the keeping up of appearances, even among themselves. Dr Allen, the family GP, was never told the truth about the family's dire finances, and neither were those house guests (like Frau Jenny's brother Edgar and the German socialist leader Ferdinand Lassalle) who, true to form, would descend and impose on the Marxes' hospitality at the least opportune moments and, often, for the most extended of periods. Marx and the elder Jenny, busily evading tradesmen and creditors, were (almost in the manner of those unfortunates that pawnbrokers called 'warm blanketeers') in and out of pawn shops with the family silver, linen and so on, but the girls throughout still had their nice dresses, their foreign-language classes and their piano lessons; appearances were also kept up in the course of Paul Lafargue's prolonged descent on the Marx household on the eve of his marriage to Laura Marx in 1868, even though (or precisely because) Lafargue at the time appeared to be rather well off. '[T]he real state of things must be anxiously hidden from him', said Marx of Lafargue. Even so, Marx took Lafargue into his confidence with respect to the latter's engagement to Laura.

You know I have sacrificed my whole fortune to the revolutionary struggle. I do not regret it. On the contrary, if I had my life over

again, I would do the same. Only I would not marry. As far as it
is in my power, I want to save my daughter from the dangerous
precipice where her mother's life was dashed to pieces

Six years earlier, Marx had confided in a letter to Engels that 'My
wife says she wishes she were with her children in her grave, and I
really cannot blame her, for the humiliations, sufferings and horrors
which we have had to go through are really indescribable.'[11]

The following year, 1863, provoked a telling lapse or want of
feeling on Marx's part when Engels's partner, Mary Burns, died in
Manchester and when Marx's condolences, made all too obviously
en passant in the midst of a letter bemoaning his own plight,
jeopardized and came close to ruining what had been a close
friendship between the two, a friendship which, it must be said,
had also been financially beneficial to Marx. 'To you', said a deeply
offended Engels, 'it seemed a suitable moment for the display of
the superiority of your own frigid way of thinking.' He added that
any one of his other friends had shown him more sympathy and
friendship than Marx had or than he, Engels, could have expected.
Marx's retraction, which was rather slow in coming, averted
disaster but was frank (and even self-pitying) rather than contrite.[12]
But the friendship was repaired, and endured.

In 1864 the Marx family moved again, around the corner to
1 Modena Villas off Haverstock Hill, on the strength, this time,
of a double inheritance, from Wilhelm Wolff (the old comrade
known as 'Lupus') as well as from Marx's mother, along with
Engels's newfound ability – he was now a partner in the family
firm in Manchester – to settle £200 per annum on the household.
Thus it was that 'in the front room first floor of Modena Villa',
as Marx's daughter Jenny later recalled in a letter to Ludwig
Kugelmann, 'I can always find my dear Mohr [Marx]. I cannot
express to you how lonely I feel when separated from him, and
he tells me that he also missed me very much and that during my

The Marx family's London home at 1 Modena Villas (later renamed 1 Maitland Park Road), Belsize Park. In 1875 the family moved to no. 41 and remained there until after Marx's and Jenny's deaths. Engels lived a few minutes walk away in Regent's Park Road from 1870 onwards.

absence he buries himself in his den . . . Though married, my heart is as chained as ever it was to the spot where my Papa is, and life elsewhere would not be life to me.' Paul Lafargue's *Reminiscences* contain a description of Marx's study:

It was on the first floor, flooded by light from a broad window that looked out on to the park. Opposite the window and on either side of the fireplace the walls were lined with bookshelves filled with books and stacked up to the ceiling with newspapers and manuscripts. Opposite the fireplace on one side of the window were two tables piled up with papers, books, and newspapers; in the middle of the room, well into the light,

Marx and daughter Jenny.

stood a small, plain desk (three foot by two) and a wooden armchair; between the armchair and the bookcase, opposite the window, was a leather sofa on which Marx used to lie down for a rest from time to time. On the mantelpiece were more books, cigars, matches, tobacco boxes, paperweights and photographs of Marx's daughters and wife, Wilhelm Wolff and Frederick Engels . . .[13]

It was not until 1868 – the year Marx's second daughter, Laura, married Paul Lafargue – that Engels was able to settle upon Marx a regular income of £350 per annum, starting in 1869. Marx throughout his London years made more – much more – money from gifts and bequests than from publication remittances, fees, contracts and royalties; the days were long past when bequests could be ploughed back into radical journals, as they had been, briefly, in Brussels and in the 1848–50 period in London, when Marx sunk a goodly amount of money in the short-lived *Neue Rheinische Zeitung Revue*. The Marxes' subsequent keeping up of appearances among their suburban neighbours in north London has of course long been derided by some of Marx's more comfortably situated biographers; Marx would also no doubt have been derided – this time as a poseur – had he insisted on principle that his family live like proles. There are times when you just can't win.

Mention of Lafargue adds another wrinkle to the family drama: in 1882 Marx was to say, only half-jokingly, of his French sons-in-law: 'Longuet as the last Proudhonist and Lafargue as the last Bakuninist! The devil take them both!' Yet it was he, not the devil, who had taken them in. Both Lafargue and Charles Longuet, who was to marry Marx's daughter Jenny (the two were engaged in 1872), were to be Communards. (Longuet was a member of the Council of the Commune and editor of its official newspaper; the Lafargues were also fugitives from the Commune.) Marx, who was not always the most tolerant of men, had his political differences from each of his eldest daughters' suitors, who were welcomed into the family nonetheless. Eleanor's would-be suitor, Hippolyte-Prosper-Olivier Lissagaray, by contrast, was not similarly welcomed, even though Marx was to have the highest opinion of Lissagaray's history of the Paris Commune; Marx's political esteem for Lissagaray did not stop him from regarding its author as a quite unsuitable consort for his favourite daughter.[14] Marx's hospitality – his open door, which had been well known among the *quarante-huitards,* was opened again for refugees from the Paris Commune – had its limits.

One particular piece of scurrility about the Marx ménage will not pass unmentioned here. This is the rumour that Marx fathered an illegitimate son, Freddy or Freddie Demuth, in 1851 by the family servant, Helene Demuth (also known variously as 'Lenchen', 'Nim' or 'Nimmy'). Today, the story of Marx's fathering Freddy is common in biographical accounts. But it is nowhere to be encountered in any account published before the 1960s, and this is in itself cause for suspicion. It is a fishy chronology that begins only in the (shall we say) politically charged decade of the 1960s, when much mud was thrown in more than one direction, in the evident hope that some of it would stick. Why did this particular piece of character assassination – for this is what it is – come to the surface only then, and at no earlier time? Who or what was its actual source? The latter question admits of a clear and certain answer, which casts light on the former. A letter, dated 2–4 September 1898, written by Louise Kautsky, *née* Strasser, Karl Kautsky's estranged wife – who never met any of the Marxes, though Karl Kautsky did, and addressed, supposedly, to August Bebel (whose silence about it is resounding) spins a tale straight from the pages of Victorian melodrama at its most Gothic. It is a tale of deathbed revelations on the part of Engels to Marx's daughter Eleanor to the effect that he, Engels, had assumed the paternity of Freddy Demuth, in order to spare Marx – who, according to Louise's account of what Engels said to Eleanor,

Helene Demuth, housekeeper and mainstay of the Marx household.

was Freddy's 'real' father – any embarrassment. Note if you will that the sole (third-hand) source of this supposed 'revelation' is Louise Kautsky, not Eleanor. The date on the letter that was supposedly sent to Bebel is six months after Eleanor's own death, prior to which she had said nothing to anyone except Louise Kautsky (if we are to believe Louise Kautsky) about any of this. Note also, if you will, that Louise Kautsky sat on this story – which no other person so much as mentioned, to which no other person even adverted either before or after the deaths of Marx, Engels, Eleanor or Lenchen herself – for *52 years* before her own death in 1950. My sense is that this entire fable about the lecherous Marx – who, if anything, was uxorious in reality – either (at one extreme) strains credulity, or (at the other) stinks to high heaven. It certainly would not pass muster in a court of law. Not to put too fine a point on matters, there is not one shred of actual evidence in the surviving correspondence of anyone except Louise Kautsky – and this source is dicey – that Karl Marx was Freddy Demuth's father, but there exist ample grounds for suspicion of the motives of those who with malicious glee spread the damaging rumour that he was so. It is striking that rumours of Marx's having fathered Freddy are conspicuous by their absence from any source at the time the dastardly act was supposedly committed (1851); the German and French exile communities in London were rife with gossip and intrigue, and Marx was not lacking for enemies. That not one of these levelled so damaging an accusation at the time beggars belief.[15] Normally in Victorian times servant girls who inconveniently got pregnant (no matter by whom) were summarily dismissed. The Marx family, as we might expect was made of more enlightened stuff. Lenchen, far from never darkening Marx's door again, was so much part of the family that even though she outlived those whose names are also on the commemorative slab in Highgate Cemetery – Jenny von Westphalen, Karl Marx, Harry Longuet, their grandson (1876–1883) – she was buried in the same grave as Karl and Jenny. This, if I may venture an opinion, speaks well of them all.

In view of all the impecuniousness and heartbreak that scarred his domestic circumstances, it is a wonder that Marx managed to do any work at all, let alone the prodigious amount he actually accomplished throughout his 34 years in London, a city Marx came to regard straightforwardly as a 'favourable vantage point . . . for the observation of bourgeois society', Britain at large being 'the demiurge of the bourgeois cosmos'. Eleanor alone among the Marx daughters was self-consciously to identify herself as a radical Londoner and a 'Jewess'. Her sisters Jenny and Laura merely shared Eleanor's dread of having to live in Germany, to which London was an available substitute rather than a city positively to be championed.

To begin with, Marx's political and theoretical concerns in London continued to centre on France, for reasons that should detain us. One of them is that in the course of *The Eighteenth Brumaire of Louis Bonaparte*, Marx describes the French small-holding peasants in terms that are chilling for some classes – or by extension for some groups – and not for others: 'They cannot represent themselves, they must be represented' (*Sie können sich nicht vertreten, sie müssen vertreten werden*). The peasantry's support of the warmed-over Bonapartist regime is not the expression of a genuine class interest, since no real class formation had taken place in the instance of the French peasantry. Marx's characterization of the smallholding (*parzellen*) peasants – who are in his opinion every-thing an authentic social class is not – deserves citing at length.

> The smallholding peasants form a vast mass, the members of which live in similar conditions but without entering into manifold relations with one another. Their mode of production isolates them from one another instead of bringing them into mutual sociability. Their isolation is increased by France's bad means of communication and by the poverty of the peasants. Their field of production, the smallholding, admits of no division of labour in its cultivation, no application of science, and, therefore, no diversity of development, no variety of talent, no wealth of social relationships. Each individual peasant family is almost self-sufficient; it itself directly produces the major part of its consumption and thus acquires its means of life more through exchange with nature than in exchange with society. A smallholding, a peasant and his family; alongside them another smallholding, another peasant and another family. A few score of these make up a village, and a few score of villages make up a *Département*. In this way, the great mass of the French nation is formed by simple addition of homo-logous magnitudes, much as potatoes in a sack form a sack of

potatoes. In so far as millions of families live under economic conditions that separate their mode of life, their interests and their culture from those of the other classes, and put them in a hostile opposition to the latter, they form a class. In so far as there is a merely local interconnection among these small-holding peasants, and the identity of their interests begets no community, no national bond and no political organization among them, they do not form a class. They are consequently incapable of enforcing their class interests in their own name . . . Their representative (*Vertreter*) must at the same time appear as their master, as an authority over them, as an unlimited governmental power that protects them against other classes and sends them rain and sunshine from above.[16]

Marx's sarcasm is evident; his polemic – which, as ever, is not just polemic – is no passing figure of speech:

the mortgage that the peasant has on heavenly possessions guaranteed the mortgage that the bourgeoisie has on peasant possessions . . . Re-established bourgeois rule in France re-established papal rule in Rome.

Marx, by way of accounting for Louis-Napoléon's foray into Italian politics, is here joining the dots with some skill. In the following century Hannah Arendt was to present social atomization as the outcome of authoritarian rule; Marx by contrast had presented social atomization as the *precondition* of authoritarianism. The *Brumaire* speaks of the dispersion, dislocation, displacement, interchangeability and dispensability of persons who appear to be rooted organically to one spot, their 'own' little plot of soil. The smallholding peasants are fused into a negative uniformity, as in Jean-Paul Sartre's related notion of 'seriality', and are not capable of uniting themselves into a positive unity. Thus it is not just the privileged who have a vested interest in the preservation of the status quo, though it is only the privileged who *enjoy* it. Ironically, it is also those who are among the status quo's worst-off victims who are most tightly locked into it and form its very basis.

The back-reference here is arguably to Hegel's depiction of civil society in the *Philosophy of Right*, where differentiation without unity reigns supreme, where other people are dealt with or engaged with, but in a purely formal manner, where relations among people are abstract, partial, incomplete, unsubstantiated, where the identities of those with whom we deal exist but do not matter. In Hegel's civil society people encounter others reflectively, calculatingly, outwardly, indirectly. People relate, but only as their purposes, interests and pursuits – all of which, it goes without saying, are individualistically defined – relate. And a society of interchangeability – by extension from Hegel's argument as well as from Marx's – is no society at all.

The difference between Hegel and Marx in this particular connection is however that while Hegel's depiction of civil society has its positive side, Marx's depiction of the French peasants is unrelentingly negative, deleterious through and through. Indeed, Marx's distinction between the *Klasse für sich* and the *Klasse an sich* is nowhere better expressed and nowhere put to better use than in his depiction of the French peasantry. The peasantry would have to believe itself to be a *Klasse für sich* if it were to become one, and there is quite simply no basis among its members for such a belief. As things stand, they cannot *represent* themselves because their very identity as peasants is imposed upon them from without and on high. There is a logic of displacement at work in Marx's *Brumaire*. At the most obvious level Louis-Napoléon, the nephew, is the *Ersatzmann* for Napoléon Bonaparte, the uncle. In pointing this out we are by no means done with Marx's employment of the verb *vertreten*, for this is not the only verb in the German language for 'represent'. There is also *darstellen*, which is generally used inter

alia in accounts of the theatre (*Paul Robeson stellt Othello dar*).
While a *Stellvertreter* in a court of law would speak for, take the
place of, the plaintiff, acting on his behalf and effectively silencing
him or her at one and the same time, a *Darsteller* is an actor, a
Darstellung an exhibition, presentation or performance. *darstellen*
also has a more philosophical meaning: to represent in the sense
of appearing to perception in an immediate way; to describe,
display, exhibit, present or produce. It is the verb Marx uses in
his celebrated characterization of 'The Fetishism of Commodities'
in *Capital*. 'Appears as' or 'plays the role of' might serve as a direct,
straightforward translation of *stellt . . . dar*, and this is a more
important point than might initially be supposed. To juxtapose
to the *Brumaire* Marx's other significant diagnosis of French
politics prior to the Commune, *The Civil War in France*, is to
notice something quite striking. This is that *Class Struggles*, which
deals with the February revolution of the French of 1848, which
preceded the *coup d'état* with which Louis-Napoléon seized power
in December 1851, is chock-a-block with theatrical imagery – the
stage, the wings, the gallery, costuming and so on. Marx, we may
surmise, took care to cap this merely theatrical imagery – which in
itself had been damaging enough – with another kind of imagery
presaged in the very first line of the *Brumaire*, an imagery this time
of masquerade, farce, travesty and *Grand Guignol*. ('Hegel remarks
somewhere that all facts and personages of great importance in
world history occur, as it were, twice. He forgot to add: the first
time as tragedy, the second as farce.' Marx believed that the
farcical nature of the nephew – who was in truth an unprepos-
sessing figure if ever there was one – does nothing to diminish
or dispel the tragic dimension of the uncle, who was a disaster
of another kind for the French nation.)

In the *Brumaire* the term 'representation' glistens with a myriad
of meanings as Marx's argument runs its course. Marx eschews
darstellen in the *Brumaire*, but does not simply substitute the verb

vertreten, for the German language also has on offer the verb *vorstellen*, to represent in the sense of 'to imagine', but with a degree of self-consciousness or reflexivity. (The difference can be put in the following way: if Ian McKellen plays Hamlet, the verb would be *darstellen*; if, however, Hamlet himself represents indecision, the verb would be *vorstellen*.) *Vorstellen* is what the French peasantry would have to do, but are incapable of doing, if they were to undertake the mental leap from being but an objectively given *Klasse an sich* to a subjectively self-creating *Klasse für sich*. It is because they cannot take this *salto mortale* (*hic Rhodus, hic salta*) that *vertreten* is to continue to apply to them

Marx's *Brumaire* deals with the 'social origins of dictatorship and democracy' (if I may here purloin the title of an excellent book by Barrington Moore Jr [17]), and suggests that that dictatorship and formal democracy were much closer together in mid-nineteenth century France (and, perhaps, beyond its boundaries) than we might be comfortable believing. Constitutional representative democracy will be but a hollow shell, form without content – it will be 'abstract', that is to say, in the Hegelian sense of the world – unless steps are taken to deal with the problem of economic inequality. If this is not done, the wealthy – then as now – will simply hijack the system by concentrating wealth and power in their own hands.

The *Brumaire* traces out the lineaments of a delusionary politics in which a class politics is masked or disguised by the formal language of equality or, worse still, by the triad of *Liberté, Egalité, Fraternité*. What Marx termed 'a modern mythology whose gods are Liberty, Equality and Fraternity' is a mythology Marx had attacked in the 1840s, as we have seen, and which was to raise its head again within the German Social Democratic Party in the 1870s, thus helping call forth Marx's 'Critique of the Gotha Programme'. Politics in the French Second Empire – and not just in the French Second Empire – was strung out on the same slogan.

Louis-Napoléon, whose 1851 *coup d'etat* Marx satirized in the *Eighteenth Brumaire*.

Louis-Napoléon appeared to win an election, then proceeded to restrict the franchise the moment that the state and security of property (that holy of holies) appeared to be threatened. The electorate was then extended so that Louis-Napoléon might secure the support of the smallholding peasants; this extension offended the Party of Order, who appeared to support the Second Empire but in reality undermined and subverted it by wishing to treat its President as their puppet, as someone to take the blame once things went wrong. But it is the would-be puppet and his Bohemian entourage of ne'er-do-wells –the *lazzaroni* – who get the last laugh, at the expense and in the face of the French nation and of nineteenth-century civilization at large.

To mention the Party of Order, the *lazzaroni* and the small-holding peasants is to recall something Marx had been stressing ever since *The German Ideology* and *The Poverty of Philosophy*: that it is class struggle, and not just class structure, that is the key to understanding the Second Empire and, by extension, bourgeois society in general. The distinction of the *Klasse für sich* from the *Klasse an sich* means among other things that you cannot simply derive the former from the latter, that you cannot map class struggle on to class structure, just like that. Struggle grows out of structure under the right enabling conditions, and Marx was careful to insinuate himself as a theorist on the cusp of the difference between the two. He wrote his *Brumaire* in 1852, a year when Louis-Napoléon could still have been undone and deposed, and to this end tried hard, but in vain, to have the *Brumaire* published in France also.

Capital

It is Marx's desire to engage with and undermine an ideological mode of argument that helps explain 'the critique of political economy' he characterized as his life's work and which he gave as the subtitle to his magnum opus, *Capital*. The 'work in question', Marx said in 1858, 'is the critique of economic categories or . . . the system of bourgeois economy critically presented. It is the presentation of the system and, at the same time, through the presentation, its critique.'[18] It was in other words to take the form of a critical outline of capitalism alongside a critique of the concepts, the theoretical frameworks, that were said to justify, legitimize or be appropriate to capitalism. Marx sought 'to make petrified conditions dance by singing to them their own melody'. He thought that unmasking the political economists' precepts, which conceal as well as reveal, would lay bare the real workings

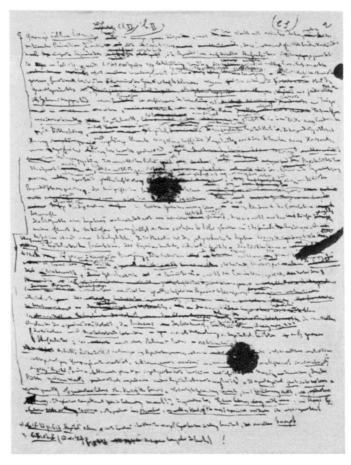

A page from the manuscript of *Capital*.

of the economy. Marx's *Economic and Philosophic Manuscripts* of
1844 already provided a prolegomenon:

> Just as we have found the concept of private property by analysis
> from the concept of estranged, alienated labor, in the same way
> every category of political economy can be evolved with the help

of these two factors [private property and alienated labour]; and we shall find again in each category, e.g. trade, competition, capital, money, only a definite and developed expression of these first foundations.[19]

And find this expression Marx did – not because of error or bias on the part of any particular political economist, but because of political economy's basic concepts and presuppositions, all of which bore a special relationship to the capitalist form of production. It is in this sense that 'the anatomy of bourgeois society may be sought in political economy'.

Political economy understands the common life of man, the self-activating human essence and mutual reintegration towards generic and truly human life, in the form of exchange and commerce. Society, says Destutt de Tracy, is a series of multilateral exchanges. It is constituted by this movement of multilateral integration. Society, says Adam Smith, is a commercial enterprise. Each of its members is a merchant. It is evident that political economy establishes an alienated form of social intercourse as the essential, original and definitive human form.[20]

Most modern economists' accounts of what they call 'Marxian economics' centre upon the view that Marx vitiated his economic analysis by virtue of having inherited, uncritically, a labour theory of value from the classical political economists. The logical consistency and strength of Marx's subsequent analysis is then generally admitted. From the labour theory of value and his concept of the commodity Marx derived his concepts of use value and exchange value. From the distinction between these two concepts he derived the concept of surplus value, which in turn he distinguished from profit, which forms but a part of surplus value.

Surplus value in turn accounts for capital accumulation; for changes over time in the 'organic composition' of capital (that is, the ratio of human labour to machinery, as machine labour or automation begins to displace or dislodge human labour); and for the tendential law of the 'falling rate of profit' (rate being distinguished from amount) which will lead – other countervailing tendencies to one side – to periodic crises in production, crises that will generally fall short of being catastrophic for capitalism at large.

This conventional account of Marx's procedure rightly allows that Marx's argument is logically consistent and also takes on board Marx's own admission of countervailing tendencies (technological innovation, separation of control over the forces of production from ownership of them) that may stave off, for a while, the demise of capitalism. Even so, Marx's ostensible premise, the labour theory of value he is said to have adopted uncritically from the political economists, is regarded either as a puzzle or as being inherently assailable.

Few modern economists would spend time worrying, as Marx did, about what a commodity is. They would simply set about analysing the production, distribution and exchange of goods, bracketing the question – which was central to Marx – of why, with the onset of capitalism, such products became identified as commodities in the first place. Similarly, few modern economists would expend much effort in thinking about what value is. Many of them, indeed, would these days regard value as a 'metaphysical' concept having no analytical purchase in the 'real world'. As far as modern economists are concerned, the price of goods on the market has to do simply with supply and demand, and a well-formed economic statement about this or any other figuration is one that can be formulated in exact, mathematical terms. 'Political economy' is generally regarded today as having been a precursor or presentiment of modern economics, the latter having taken its cue from the marginalist revolution. The modern science of economics is then said to have set forth an unambiguous, mathematically based focus on pricing, as opposed to 'political economy's' more 'philosophical' questionings about the nature of value, money, profit and so forth.

The marginalist approach, which was given formulation, we should remember, by Sir Edward Stanley Jevons (whose *Theory of Political Economy* was first published in 1871) and others within Marx's lifetime, seemed to Marx to raise a lot of important questions. If indeed we are to be exact, what are we to be exact *about*? Value was a category the political economists had worried over before connecting it (as they all did) with labour. The starting point of Marx's analysis was not at all an uncritical espousal of this same connection, but the recognition that value cannot be regarded as a simple expression of labour, because labour could be regarded much more straightforwardly as the source of wealth, and wealth, like labour, is a much older category than capital or capitalism. Value, on the other hand, is a historically specific expression of a historically specific form of labour. As a social convention that is specific to capitalism, value is a particular form of wealth that is materialized in the commodity. How and why the old concept of wealth got displaced or countermanded by the new, original concept of value, and why this happened when it happened and at no earlier time – these are important questions to Marx. The question of why this substitution took place when it took place and at no other time would surely be of interest to more recent economists too, if these economists were to show the slightest interest in the history of their own discipline. If these questions are not raised, capitalism cannot be understood genetically, as it emerged at a particular historical juncture. If capitalism is not understood as it arose, its own historical specificity cannot be accounted for, and capitalism will falsely and uncritically be understood as the universal norm and standard by which all earlier modes of production should be judged. It is then likely that these earlier modes of production will, in their turn, become the pivot, the be-all and end-all of economic activity at large, as well as of economic speculation of any kind. This indeed is the trap into which the political economists themselves duly fell. While it is unlikely that more modern economists will themselves, by extension, fall into this same trap in the same way, the trap itself – the trap, that is, of falsely absolutizing capitalism as the be-all and end-all of human existence – has widened considerably over the span of time that separates us from Marx. All the more reason why Marx should still throw down, or cast across this span, his own particular gauntlet.

Marx's economic analysis is designed to show (inter alia) that '[n]ature does not produce on the one hand owners of money or commodities, and on the other men possessing nothing but their own labour power', that '[t]his relation has no basis in natural history, nor does it have a social basis common to all periods of human history. It is clearly the result of a past historical development, the product of many economic revolutions, of the extinction of a whole series of older formations of social production.'[21] Accordingly Marx's analysis employs the historically specific concepts of use value, exchange value and surplus value. Briefly put, use value, which simply means that there exists some demand for whatever gets produced, is in no way specific to commodity production or to capitalism. Use value exists whenever products get produced, and production as such is in no way specific to capitalism as a singular mode of production. It is not the production of goods or products that characterizes capitalism, but the production and exchange of commodities. Exchange value, which Marx sometimes, confusingly, calls 'value', on the other hand, is specific to commodity production and to capitalism in a particular way. The distinction between use value and exchange value is akin to the difference between material content and social form. Exchange value cannot be formulated or calculated on the basis of use value. Anything produced for purposes of exchange will have exchange value, which does not displace or annul use value, but complements or augments it. Anything having exchange value must also have use value, otherwise it would be unsaleable. But the reverse is not the case: exchange value characterizes capitalism in particular (though, like money, it may exist in the interstices of earlier modes of production too) and not production in general. Exchange value, that is to say, cannot be derived from use value, only superadded to it, as a supplement. But exchange value can, all the same, effectively *displace* use value in the sense that 'use values must . . . never be treated as the immediate aim of the capitalist', who produces use value in order to gain exchange value. What happens under capitalism is that commodities, in order to meet demand or 'realize' their use values, must first be exchanged against or in terms of other commodities. Exchange value then becomes the fulcrum, pivot or motivation of any capitalist transaction and the determining motive of economic activity at large. Marx kick-starts the first volume of *Capital* with the concept of the commodity by immediately juxtaposing and counterposing its two defining aspects, use value and exchange value, which are not just distinguished one from the other as concepts, but are regarded throughout in relation to one another. Under capitalism, and under capitalism alone, you simply can't have one without the other.

Interestingly, even though Marx is conventionally labelled a 'materialist', the materiality of the commodity may be its least significant feature. 'The commodity form, and the value relation of the products of labour with which it appears, have absolutely no connection with the physical nature of the commodity.' Again,

> not an atom of matter enters into the objectivity of commodities as values . . . commodities possess an objective character as values only in so far as they are all expressions of an identical social substance, human labour . . . their objective character as values

is therefore purely social. From this it follows self-evidently that that it can only appear in the social relation between commodity and commodity.[22]

(This formulation sounds paradoxical, and we will return to it presently). Value itself is both immaterial and objective. It is a social, that is to say a conventional relation, and as such cannot be touched or felt or experienced by anyone directly. Yet social relations have objective effects; in capitalism immateriality and objectivity (like use value and exchange value) relate in a particular way.

The ultimate commodity – the commodity of commodities, if you will – as Marx had already suggested in the *Economic and Philosophic Manuscripts*, is money. It cannot be directly consumed, but despite this, money vastly extends and enhances the scope of exchange. ('As the hart pants after fresh water, so pants [the capitalist's] soul after money, the only wealth.') Under capitalist conditions money serves both as an index of the value of all other commodities and as capital, that is as self-expanding exchange value. Yet, to reiterate, exchange value throughout remains a purely conventional attribute of a commodity, having nothing to do with what that commodity is supposed to be *for*. Exchange value refers not to the nature or being or use of a commodity but simply to its social form. Nevertheless it is the production of more exchange value, and not the production of more goods, that is privileged under capitalism and becomes the fulcrum of transaction. The productive forces expand, and use values get realized, to be sure, but these things happen indirectly, adventitiously and in a manner that increases suffering and alienation among the working population. This means that a severe reversal has set in, and will continue to be self-reinforcing, like the accumulation of capital itself, unless the chain of causality be broken, as Marx thinks it can. Human relationships have in the meantime become phenomena of the market, which is itself subject to no conscious social control.

Humanity, as in the 1844 *Manuscripts*, is busily, indeed obsessively, defeating its own purpose(s).

To approach the phenomenon of value from another direction, the political economists had recognized that it is the character of labour that gives the clue to the character of value, for value has no other source. Even skilled labour is in Marx's estimation nothing other than simple labour 'with a higher specific gravity'. What Marx now throws into the mix is crucial. Abstract, undifferentiated labour, labour that is fundamentally meaningless, what Marx calls 'labour in general, labour *sans phrase*', is the only possible source of exchange value. It is important to the capitalist labour process that the worker be able to turn himself to a variety of tasks without undue difficulty, that he or she be able to move easily and unproblematically from one occupational slot to any other. What could make work personal or distinctive is, like use value, no longer of any economic importance. What is by contrast of economic importance, what is in fact all-important, is that each and every act of labour be measurable against any other act of labour, by the clock, or in terms of units of output per unit of time. As we had occasion to observe in our discussion of Marx's Brussels writings, what Marx calls 'labour power', thus defined (or reduced), tells us as much about any labourer as horse-power does a horse.

Just as exchange value abstracts from the specific qualities or characteristics of goods and products, treating these as 'commodities' in an abstract quantitative ratio, so too labour power will express nothing about the personalities, gifts, aptitudes, inclinations or preferences of any individual worker. In Plato's *Republic* the division of labour means that people who are differently endowed have appropriately different functions to perform; in the capitalist division of labour, which is in reality a division of tasks, differently endowed people all do the same thing. The parallelism between exchange value and labour power would be complete, and labour would be a commodity just like any other, but for one thing – which ironically was Marx's very starting point: the uniquely generative power of human labour as such. It is contact with living labour that resuscitates the value of the dead labour that that may already be congealed in products.

> by incorporating living labour into . . . lifeless objectivity, the capitalist simultaneously transforms value, i.e. past labour in its objectified and lifeless form into capital . . . an animated monster which begins to 'work' as if its body were by love possessed.[23]

Labour generates something beyond itself even under the most alienating of conditions. It creates and re-creates the power by which its own further exploitation is made possible and (under capitalism) likely. Humanity in the capitalist epoch has lost control of its own evolution, its own standing in the natural world.

In a society where people produce and exchange them, commodities as it were take on a life of their own and constrain those who produce them. To explain this, Marx makes an analogy to

> the misty realm of religion [where] the products of the human brain appear as autonomous figures endowed with a life of their own . . . [they appear as] independent forms standing in relations among themselves [as well as] with men. So it is in the commodity world with the products of the human hand . . .[24]

The fetish-character of commodities derives from the 'peculiar social character of the labour that produces them' – a character that is 'peculiar' in that producers relate significantly with other producers only through the exchange of the commodities they produce. Commodities are produced in the first instance not because of their usefulness but primarily for the sake of exchange against other commodities, and this gives objects something important in common over and above the uses to which they may be put. It gives them exchangeability, a common value-character which comes to manipulate products and producers alike.

The commodity is in no way a self-explanatory concept, but it gives us an essential clue to the nature of economic reality. If human beings relate significantly only as their commodities relate, then human relations are reduced to the continuum of exchange relationships. 'Under capitalism the relations of production appear to individuals as what they are, material relations between persons and social relations between things.' Marx saw in the production and exchange of commodities an important manifestation of alienation in capitalist society. In the words of David Harvey's paraphrase of Marx's argument,

> the capitalist produces and reproduces the worker as the active but alienated subject capable of producing value. And this . . . is the fundamental socially necessary condition for the survival and maintenance of a capitalist mode of production.[25]

Capital describes 'the bewitched, distorted and upside-down world haunted by Monsieur le Capital and Madame la Terre, who are at the same time social characters and mere things'. The book is replete with references to phenomena that are invisible, concealed or veiled, to symbols, secrets, fantasies, enigmas, riddles, most prominent among which is the commodity itself, which is variously described as mysterious or hieroglyphic. Its need for decipherment stems in part from the commodity's character as a concept, which refers to real, tangible objects but does so in a particular way. If commodities and their value are intangible, they are not for this reason purely symbolic or imaginary. They affect the way we act and think and are in this way practical concepts – practical in very much the same sense as ideology might be said to be practical: having practical effects or issue. Products of labour, things, objects, become and are treated as commodities, 'sensuous things that are

Marx in the 1860s.

at the same time supersensible or social'.[26] Without this operative, enabling assumption the capitalist economy could not and (Marx hastened to add) would not persist.

The 'fetishism of commodities' is designed to tell us something about the commodity: that it is mysterious and conventional at the same time. It is also designed to tell us something about fetishism, the attribution of human attributes to inanimate objects: that this will be exploitative and oppressive unless we can shake ourselves free from its hold. The state, law, the Church, the commodity – all can in principle operate as fetishes, unless they are unmasked practically. Things attain a life of their own and control their makers' lives if and only if their makers remain content with adapting themselves and making themselves relevant to a world they have created – a world whose revolutionary overthrow will also, at the same time, be an act of conscious reappropriation of what humanity had unconsciously alienated away. The argument here is altogether continuous with what Marx had said in the *Economic and Philosophic Manuscripts*. To identify wage labour with labour is to identify alienation with objectification and to make the supersession of alienation inconceivable. Marx's whole point, in *Capital* as in the *Manuscripts*, is that its supersession is eminently conceivable, not to mention highly urgent.

In 1859 Marx summarized what we would now call his 'methodology' in a 'Preface' whose importance ranks alongside that of his 'Theses on Feuerbach' (which, like *The German Ideology*, remained unpublished during his lifetime). The central paragraph of this 'Preface' deserves quoting at length.

The general result at which I arrived and which, once won, served as the guiding thread for my studies, can be briefly formulated as follows: In the social production of their life, men enter into definite relations that are indispensable and independent of their will, relations of production which correspond to a definite stage of development of their material productive forces. The sum total of these relations of production constitutes the economic structure of society, the real foundation, on which arises a legal and political superstructure and to which correspond definite forms of social consciousness. The mode of production of material life conditions the social, political and intellectual life process in general. It is not the consciousness of men that determines their being but, on the contrary, their social being that determines their consciousness. At a certain stage of their development, the material productive forces of society come into conflict with the existing relations of production, or – what is but a legal expression for the same thing – with the property relations within which they had been at work hitherto. From forms of development of the productive forces these relations turn into their fetters. Then begins an epoch of social revolution. With the change of the economic foundations the entire immense superstructure is more or less rapidly transformed. In considering such transformations a distinction should always be made between the material transformation of the economic conditions of production, which can be determined with the precision of natural science, and the legal, political, religious, aesthetic, or philosophic – in short, ideological forms in which men become conscious of this conflict and fight it out. Just as our opinion of an individual is not based on what he thinks of himself, so can we not judge of such a period of transformation by its own consciousness; on the contrary, this consciousness must be explained rather from the contradictions of material life, from the existing conflict between the social productive forces and the relations of production . . .[27]

The reason I am dealing with Marx's earlier 1859 'Preface' to *A Contribution to the Critique of Political Economy* after having given an account of some of the salient later arguments of volume I of *Capital* (1867) is that the 'Preface' has often been misinterpreted, while the arguments of *Capital* are by and large quite continuous with it and can cast light on where Marx was tending eight years prior to getting his magnum opus into shape. This is not to deny that the 'Preface' is as difficult a short text as Marx ever produced. It is difficult not because it takes the form of cryptic aphorisms (as the 'Theses on Feuerbach' had) but because of the compressed nature of the summary he provides. Because it is compressed and telescoped, each sentence is self-contained in relation to its surrounding sentences; at the same time, however, Marx's categories ('economic structure', 'real foundations', 'economic conditions of production', the 'social basis of production', 'social being') are near-synonymous and overlap with one another. Each category refers and is meant to refer to the others. All of the above-listed categories include the social relations of production (the class structure) *and* the (material and technological) forces of production or productive forces. All these taken together constitute the 'base', which is then related to the 'superstructure' of society. The 'economic structure of society', its 'real basis', is not in any obvious sense a material category; it contains social relations of production – relations among human beings – as well as forces of production, which are in large measure inanimate objects. A mode of production (feudalism, capitalism) is a relationship between forces of production and relations of production, a relationship between material and technological content and social form. Capitalism as a mode of production constantly revolutionizes the forces of production, but these expanding forces are going to clash with the (absolutely or relatively) contracting relations of production. Capacity to produce expands; ownership of the means of production contracts. The result is asymmetry, maladjustment, and this is not accidental but built-in. Relations of production, if these are to endure, must promote, and not hinder, the development of productive forces, and this is what capitalist relations of production cannot do. Forces here contradict relations by outstripping them, and relations become confining or restraining, a 'fetter' or 'integument' which is then 'burst asunder'. One of the best illustrations of how forces and relations of production relate in a society undergoing change was provided by Marc Bloch in his description of 'the burgesses' in *Feudal Society*. This too deserves to be quoted at length.

> Essentially the burgess lived by commerce. He derived his subsistence from the difference between the price at which he bought and the price at which he sold; or between the capital lent and the amount of repayment. And since the legality of such intermediate profit . . . was denied by the theologians and its nature ill-understood by knightly society, his code of conduct was in flagrant conflict with prevailing moral notions. For his part, as a speculator in real estate he found the feudal restrictions on his landed property intolerable. Because his business had to be handled rapidly and, as it grew, continued to set new legal problems, the delays, the complications, the archaism of the traditional judicial procedures exasperated him. The multiplicity of authorities governing the town itself offended him as obstacles to the proper control of business transactions and as an insult to the solidarity of his class. The diverse immunities enjoyed by his ecclesiastical or knightly neighbours seemed to him so many hindrances to the free pursuit of profit. On the roads which he ceaselessly traversed, he regarded with equal abhorrence rapacious toll-collectors and the predatory nobles who swooped down from their castles on the merchant caravans. In short he was harassed and annoyed by almost everything in the institutions of a society in which he had as yet only a very small place. With franchises won by violence or purchased with hard cash, organized and equipped for economic expansion . . . the town

which it was his ambition to build would be as it were a foreign body in feudal society.[28]

The distinction between forces and relations of production is what enables Marx, for his part, to deny that physical production and material growth depend upon the maintenance or furthering of capitalism. Marx's distinction also gives content to phenomena other theorists had noticed but were unable to explain: the disparity between the capacity of capitalist society to produce, and the inability of people in that society to consume; the social organization of production in the factory, and individual ownership of and control over the means of production; concentration of wealth and power in the hands of a few, and dispersion of ill-paid, alienated labour into the hands of the many. As Marx aphoristically put the matter in 1869, 'the Roman proletariat lived at the expense of society, while modern society lives at the expense of the proletariat'.

The 'Preface' gives voice, as most of Marx's other writings gave voice, to his sense of the enormous promise, and the actual depravity, of capitalism, and does so without either lapsing into a purely moralistic critique or subscribing to the romantic attitude that capitalism had disrupted some pre-industrial idyll. The pre-industrial worker could not conceive of rejecting his conditions of life, for he understood himself only as part of these conditions; the modern proletarian, by contrast, stands in a detached, alienated relation with his conditions of life. But it *is* a relation. If unity with the production process has been sacrificed, this can signify a gain in autonomy, not a loss to be lamented. Capitalism socializes the productive process, collectivizes labour and develops the productive capabilities of the human species. Even if these make only an alienated appearance, even if the outcome of their productive activities confronts human beings as alien and inimical, the possibility of further developing productive potential is at least raised by these developments. If pre-capitalist artisan labour represents an undifferentiated unity between the worker and his work, proletarianized labour under capitalist conditions signifies differentiation without unity. Once capitalist relations of production have been surpassed, the prospect is thus of differentiated unity, though Marx, who rejected in principle the possibility of 'writing . . . recipes for the cook-shops of the future', left vague the details of this unity – probably because these details would in due course be worked out by those people who were in their own right to be engaged at first hand in bringing about a new and better future. It was not up to Marx to tell them how to do this, only to explain as fully as possible why it needed doing and that it could, in principle, be done.

Marx intended his 1859 schema not as a social ontology but as a 'guiding thread', a guide to further research that lays out provisionally the questions to ask when seeking to explain why societies change or fail to change. The starting point of analysis should not be the political or legal organization of society, should not be ideology or consciousness, and should not be the level of technology attained by the society in question. (Marxism – in so far as it has anything to do with what Marx wrote – is not technological determinism. Technology functions within a social context; its ultimate source is human labour and inventiveness, but what makes it count is the character of the production process.) Marx is setting out his priorities and indicating the direction research should take. He wishes to investigate 'the material conditions of life' and dig beneath its surface manifestations in order to lay bare 'the anatomy of civil society' in the bourgeois epoch. All of Marx's various forays into broader historical questions were subsidiary, if complementary, to this aim.

While this is not the place for the most painstakingly detailed examination of the structure of the three volumes of *Capital* (and of *Theories of Surplus Value*, which has been called the fourth volume of *Capital* even though in most editions it is three-volumes-long in its own right) the point does need to be made that Marx's overall enterprise was multifaceted and enormously ambitious. Volume II confronts and plays out what volume I had held constant for the purposes of argument: the difficulties that arise in the quest for markets, for without these capitalist accumulation and circulation will not be able to proceed apace. Volume II also holds constant what volume I had developed and played out: the extraction of absolute and relative surplus value, shifts in technology and in the value of labour power. Volume III's optic is the inevitability of crisis (which arguably is where we today come in). What is important to Marx's arguments throughout *Capital* is their motility, their stress on process and their kinetic quality. Marx speaks not about labour but about labour power; capital itself is not an object but a process. Throughout, relations are emphasized rather than stand-alone principles. Just as marked is the number of echoes found in *Capital* of ideas first given expression in the pages of the *Economic and Philosophic Manuscripts* of 1844. The idea of a metabolism between mankind and nature which capitalism subverts and betrays is a prominent example, but there are many more. These span the *Manuscripts, Capital* and many works in between, prominently including the 1859 'Preface'. Marx's works, as we have had occasion to remark earlier, contain many such runnels going through them from beginning to end; each runnel is an aperture as well as a passage, and the aperture here opens up on the market as 'a very Eden of the innate rights of man', 'the exclusive realm of Freedom, Equality, Property and Bentham'.

> Freedom, because both buyer and seller of a commodity, let us say of labour power, are determined only by their own free will. They contract as free persons, who are equal before the law . . . Equality, because each enters into relations with the others as with the simple owners of commodities, and they exchange equivalent for equivalent. And Bentham, because each looks

only to his own advantage. The only force bringing them together, and putting them into relation with each other, is the selfishness, the gain, and the private interest of each. Each pays heed to himself only, and no-one worries about the others. And precisely for this reason, either in accordance with the pre-established harmony of things, or under the auspices of an omniscient providence, they all work together to their mutual advantage, for the common weal, and in the common interest.[29]

As in *The Class Struggles in France*, persons exist for each other only as representations; characters who appear on the economic stage 'are merely personifications of economic relations', and 'it is as carriers or bearers (*Träger*) of these relations that they come into contact'. As with the French peasantry in Marx's *Brumaire*, whatever attributes people display or bring to bear are not the predicates of human subjects but effects of socio-economic relations.

Except as capital personified, the capitalist has no historical value, and no right to historical existence . . . In so far as he is capital personified, his motivating force is not the acquisition and enjoyment of use values, but the acquisition and enjoyment of exchange values.

'It is not because he is a leader of industry that a man is a capitalist; on the contrary, he is a capitalist because he is a leader of industry. The leadership of industry is an attribute of capital', nothing more, nothing less. Worse yet,

because it is capital the automatic mechanism is endowed, in the person of the capitalist, with consciousness and a will. As capital, therefore, it is animated by the drive to reduce to the minimum the resistance offered by man, that obstinate yet elastic natural barrier.[30]

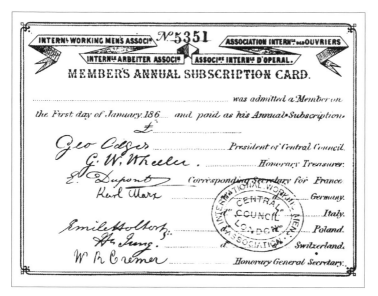

A membership card for the First International or International Working Men's Association, co signed by Marx as 'Corresponding Secretary for Germany'.

It was this same 'resistance, offered by . . . that obstinate yet elastic natural barrier' that tore Marx from his desk in 1864. The International Working Men's Association (IWMA), which came to be known as the First International, was set up that year – three years before the publication of the first volume of *Capital* – by trade unionists, but not as a purely trade unionist body. It was to be a federation across national lines of already existing associations that could unite around 'the same goal, namely, the protection, the rise, and the complete emancipation of the working class'. Its statutes and membership were non-sectarian; *ouvriériste* and Proudhonist attempts to exclude those who were not manual workers ('*pas des mains blanches, seulement les mains calleuses*') were nipped in the bud. On the other hand, the IWMA, from the outset, recruited most successfully among beleaguered, newly-threatened artisans rather than proletarians in rising, large-scale industries. Something other than (or something besides) its industrial base, that is to say, must have commended the IWMA to Marx: its internationalism and non-sectarianism. Given the circumstances of its inception, the IWMA took on and maintained a characteristic form: the freedom of manoeuvre enjoyed by politically minded trade unionists in London (where the International's General Council was headquartered) could also be enjoyed by the numerous continental refugees, *quarante-huitards* and others, who were languishing and marking time there – and who tended, by and large, to be more radical, more truculent, less reformist, gradualist and patient than the doughty English trade unionists with (or against) whom they were to work. The IWMA's inception in 1864 was in no way Marx's initiative; he did none of the groundwork setting it up. But as former head of the Communist League and co-author of the *Manifesto of the Communist Party* Marx could certainly claim some share in the IWMA's background. Once he was invited to join, he accepted eagerly and without hesitation.

The reasons for Marx's eagerness are not hard to see. Marx had long professed commitment to working-class organization that was international in scope. Having long been isolated from the 'real forces' (*wirkliche Kräfte*), as he termed them, of the labour movement in any country, Marx was quick to applaud what he saw, rightly enough, as an independent, non-sectarian initiative in the direction of working-class internationalism. 'It involved a matter where it was possible to do some important work', he wrote to Joseph Weydermeyer – the work of helping create (in the lexicon of *The Poverty of Philosophy* and beyond) a *Klasse für sich* out of the *matériel* of an existing *Klasse an sich*.[31]

Henceforward Marx was to devote a great deal of time and effort to the IWMA's cause. His dedication to the IWMA did not slacken from the moment he delivered his Inaugural Address as head of the IWMA's General Council (and drew up its 'Rules and their Preamble') in 1864 until the International's effective desuetude in 1872. In the meantime, the IWMA never really transcended or eschewed the kind of working-class sectarianism above which Marx worked hard to have it rise. Even so, it remained (as the saying goes) the only game in town when it came to international working-class politics, and the gamble that sectarianism could be put to rest for this reason alone seemed to be one that was well worth taking. But in the event, the Paris Commune (which, we should remember, no-one had predicted) did nothing to bring together the IWMA's fissiparous sects and factions; most of the English trade unionists, who were of an unimpeachably reformist disposition and had been Marx's erstwhile allies on the General Council, were appalled at the excesses not of the armed forces who butchered at least 20,000 Parisian *fédérés* city block by city block (even unto the Mur des Fédérés in Père Lachaise), but – in an egregious want of perspective – by the far lesser outrages of the *fédérés* themselves. The English adherents of the IWMA were in other words as appalled as were the bourgeoisie and the British press at the Communards' supposed excesses, which meant in the event that when Marx delivered

A street barricade set up during the 1871 Paris Commune.

The Civil War in France as an 'Address' carrying the imprimatur of the General Council of the IWMA, and when in this 'Address' he hailed the Commune as 'the glorious harbinger of a new society',[32] his standing on the General Council was very seriously eroded. Sometimes in politics it all seems to come to nothing – even though the IWMA at one level and the Commune at another continued to carry considerable symbolic and (it was devoutly to be hoped) proleptic force.

The point remains that the Commune, which was anything but one of Marx's initiatives (and about which he expressed many reservations, albeit in private) nevertheless put Marx on the horns of a dilemma. If indeed the IWMA *had* represented the 'real forces' of the European working class, how could the most celebrated working-class uprising of the nineteenth century have taken place without much more than a sidelong glance in its direction? Eleanor Marx in her obituary of her father says that 'the International was no longer practicable in its first historic form after the fall of the Commune'. True enough: but the whole truth of the matter is that the IWMA was no longer practicable after the Commune's *rise*. All the same, its brutal demise with all its butchery put Marx in an unenviable position. He could not have avoided coming out publicly in its defence (whatever his private reservations may have been), not least because of the de-institutionalization and de-alienation of political power the Commune represented and had, all too briefly, put into practice. But he knew full well what doing so would mean for his own standing on the General Council of the IWMA and, for that matter, for the IWMA itself. What Marx may not have foreseen, but what duly happened anyway, is that the press identified, indeed pinpointed, the IWMA as a 'terrorist' organization because of its presumed but non-existent connection with the Commune, and conferred upon Marx the title of 'red terrorist Doctor' because of his. (Marx declared himself to have 'the honour at this moment [1871] to be the most calumniated and most menaced man of

London'.) These unfounded accusations risked doing the IWMA – which, to reiterate, had had no more to do with the Paris Commune than had Marx himself – irreparable damage. The wheel had turned full circle cruelly. Once the IWMA, as a result of the Commune and of Marx's spirited but *ex post facto* defence of what it represented politically, had become tarred with the brush of conspiratorialism and terror, the die was well and truly cast. Marx, for the record, considered not only that conspiracy should in principle be eschewed, but also, more particularly, that the IWMA was to have been (at last) the body that could abjure and transcend conspiratorial tendencies. Combating conspiracy and terror had been one of the raisons d'être of the International all along, as the press could have seen for itself had it taken the trouble to read its rules.

The foregoing account, bare-bones and summary as it is, of the Commune and its demise raises the question of the presence (after 1868) within the IWMA of Marx's ideological rival Mikhail Bakunin (1814–1876) who, like Marx, wished to capitalize on the achievement of the *fédérés* and who had long been a thorn in Marx's side (as had Marx in his). What was at issue between the two of them can be illustrated by and through a brief excursus. Pavel Annenkov's *Literary Memoirs* recall a meeting in the 1840s at which the German revolutionary Wilhelm Weitling's utopianism so exasperated Marx that the latter hurled at Weitling the remonstrance that 'to excite the workers without giving them reasoned arguments is quite simply to deceive them. To awaken fantastic hopes can lead only to disaster, not deliverance.' My point in relating so pertinent an anecdote is not that Bakunin admired Weitling for long; his 'is not a free society', said Bakunin, 'a really live union of free people, but a herd of animals, intolerably coerced and united by force, following only material ends, utterly ignorant of the spiritual side of life'. No German revolutionary was in truth exempt from Bakunin's Teutophobia; yet the matter goes rather deeper than this – deeper, too, than Bakunin's no less evident anti-Semitism. For if Bakunin

The anarchist Mikhail Bakunin, Marx's great adversary in his last years.

had no love for Weitling, he had even less for 'theory'. It is a point of some importance that 'to excite the workers without giving them reasoned arguments' and 'to awaken fantastic hopes' was *precisely* what Bakunin set out to do.[33] Fantastic hopes, not reasoned arguments, were to Bakunin the very breath of revolution. Theory was in his eyes a 'metaphysic', which by paralysing 'fantastic hopes' paralysed revolutionary action itself. It was a mainstay of Bakunin's revolutionism that where there was a doctrine, or an intellectual construction of any kind, there lurked in the background the hated forces of centralization and the state.

How distant such views were from Marx's need not at this juncture be laboured. But the distance is not just one between views or opinions. It has been argued that Bakuninism was the last straw to break the International's back. In fact matters were rather more complicated. To appreciate these complications we must stand back and take our bearings. What distinguishes Marx's celebrated dispute with Bakunin from his earlier disagreements with anarchist theoreticians (Max Stirner in *The German Ideology* and Pierre-Joseph Proudhon in *The Poverty of Philosophy*) is the institutional setting in which it was carried on. It was no mere war of words; neither side in the contretemps produced a major theoretical defence of his position. These positions have to be reconstructed from the arguments that went back and forth within an institutional setting, arguments that thus had immediately political as well as ultimately theoretical stakes. These stakes were raised yet higher because the views that were batted back and forth involved questions about the IWMA itself – its principles, its goals, its ends, its organization: questions about what kind of body the International was to be, besides being a platform from which the views of Marx, Bakunin and others could be launched and disseminated. Marx's views about organizational and ideological questions after 1868 were formulated and broadcast in contradistinction and as an immediate response to the rival views of Bakunin and others. The important point here is that what Marx, for his part, had to contend with was not, this time, a body of doctrine having a vague if irksome appeal that was restricted behind a particular national boundary – this in the end is all that Stirner or even Proudhon had amounted to – but an anarchist *movement* having widespread appeal across international boundaries, a movement which spread most widely in areas where what was becoming known as Marxism was at its weakest. We are dealing, then, with what was a contestation in the fullest sense of the word, compared with which Marx's attacks on Stirner and Proudhon were but verbal donnybrooks. While Stirner had not taken it upon himself, and Proudhon had not deigned to reply to Marx's accusations in person or in print, Bakunin for his part suffered from no such reticence. The stakes were high for him too. Without the IWMA, we would have had Bakunin, a larger-than-life figure who was (to put matters mildly) adept at making his presence felt. But we might not have had Bakuninism as a mass movement.[34]

To say this is not however to suggest that at any point in its short history the IWMA could be described as either 'Marxist' or 'Bakuninist' in complexion. While it contained throughout its existence a powerful Marxist tendency and a growing Bakuninist upsurge that threatened to displace it, these existed alongside and among many other groups, tendencies and persuasions. These were just as characteristic as were Marxism or Bakuninism of the kind of organization the IWMA was. Unlike future Internationals, it was never intended to be ideologically monolithic. It was, rather, a fissiparous and contentious body from the word go, and could scarcely have been anything else; the Marx–Bakunin dispute was the most dramatic but by no means the only doctrinal disagreement that punctuated and animated its proceedings. All such disagreements, in the event, paled alongside (and became trumped by) the

The first congress of the First International, 1866, held in Geneva.

Paris Commune, which, to reiterate, was neither a Marxian not a Bakuninist initiative, even if both Marx and Bakunin wished, after the event, to assume its mantle and capitalize on what each of them thought the Commune represented. The Commune, its repression and its subsequent mythologization – all had an adverse effect on the IWMA, in large measure because this body had already been weakened by the Marx–Bakunin dispute.

In assessing the Marx–Bakunin dispute we should not picture its protagonists thundering at each other from the podium. The more prosaic truth of the matter is that they did not attend the same international congresses. The only one that Bakunin attended was the congress of Basel in 1869; the only one that Marx attended was the IWMA congress at The Hague in 1872, at which, with no small degree of chagrin, he and Engels delivered their bombshell, effectively killing off the IWMA by successfully proposing a disarmingly simple expedient: that the seat of its General Council be shifted or outsourced to New York. If we ask why so dramatic a move had in Marx's view become necessary, the demise of the Commune and the International provide more than enough reason.

Bakunin had at the outset of his participation taken issue with the phraseology of Marx's 'Preamble' to the rules of the IWMA, with the injunction that 'to conquer political power has . . . become the great duty of the working class.' These were words – fighting words – to which the Proudhonists, too, had taken exception, as Marx knew in advance they would. He stuck to his guns in the belief that, politically, it was more important to wean the German working class from the clammy embrace of the recently decedent Lassalle, and to cement an alliance between the General Council and representatives of the English working class, than it was to assuage the feelings of and otherwise coddle the French Proudhonists, whose base was obsolescent, whose days were numbered and whose leader's opinions had in any case never been plagued by consistency.

Marx's insertion of his fateful phrase about the conquest of political power was then a political move, though how prescient a move it was is another question. Marx could not have known at the time of its utterance that it would rile Bakuninists as well as Proudhonists; there were prior to 1868 no Bakuninists in evidence. But he must have known that any alliance between the General Council and the English on whose territory it convened (and where alone it would not be persecuted) would give the IWMA its needed ballast only if English capitalism should prove to be the wave of the future. Marx was convinced that sooner or later, in one way or another, 'the English facts reproduce themselves [or will do so] in all the industrious and progressive countries of the continent.' This prediction Marx repeated in the 'Preface' to the first volume of *Capital* in 1867, but it did nothing to endear him to Bakunin, who thought that proletarianization stifled rather than stimulated revolutionary ardour, ardour that was more likely to be met with in its primordial, igneous, elemental form among the peasant masses of non-industrialized (but European) lands – particularly those that were threatened with imminent proletarianization. Not only did the spread of Bakuninism during and after the years of the International in Switzerland, France, Italy and Spain call into question both of Marx's central assumptions; these same assumptions – about the political character of the seizure of power, and about proletarianization as the writing on the wall – were assumptions that Bakunin had reason to regard as a threat.

These differences, and the political disputes based upon them, animated, weakened and in a sense defined the IWMA. They also helped set the stage for the impact of the Paris Commune and its repression. The International never really overcame sectarianism, however much Marx may have desired that it do so. But it was nevertheless as a result of the Commune regarded by the press as the kind of underground, conspiratorial organization Bakunin would have liked it to be – with Marx, the 'red terrorist Doctor', pulling its strings, just as Bakunin had imagined (or fantasized) all along. This was to rub salt into the wound with a vengeance. The International, as a result of Marx's defence of the Commune, was tarred with the brush of conspiratorialism and terrorism at the very moment when Bakuninism looked most threatening and the International itself most prone to imploding. Marx's response was to help *dis*assemble the International at The Hague, at which point, his hopes dashed, he retreated into his study.

He did so not for the first time, but it was to be for the last. For all this, Marx in many ways continued to be his old, recognizable self. H. M. Hyndman, the British socialist who got to know Marx only late in their lives, advanced a description that sounds many a familiar echo:

> the old warrior's small, deep-sunken eyes lighted up, his heavy brow wrinkled, the broad, strong nose and face were obviously moved by passion, and he poured forth a stream of vigorous denunciation, which displayed alike the heat of his temperament and the marvelous command he possessed over our language . . . He turned from the rôle of prophet and vehement denunciator to that of the calm philosopher without any apparent effort, and I felt from the first that . . . many a long year might pass before I ceased to be a student in the presence of a master . . .[35]

The years were however to speed by. Marx's health was worsening; in 1874 he decided to follow doctor's orders and 'take the waters' at a German health spa, Carlsbad, and to apply for naturalization as a British subject beforehand. The Home Office turned down his request after hearing from Scotland Yard that Marx was 'the notorious German agitator' who 'had not been loyal to his own king and country'. (One can almost hear these words being not so much pronounced as sniffed.) Marx was subject to police surveillance at Carlsbad, a spa resort to which he repaired more than

Marx in later life.

once in his declining years, in large measure because the Anti-Socialist Laws precluded a German agitator's visiting a German spa. But at Carlsbad for once he 'did not give rise to any suspicion' in the eyes of the German police who were keeping them on him.

Marx in a sense was by now having the worst of all possible worlds. There was no longer an International: he evidently saw more point in finishing *Capital* than in continuing to wear himself out in pursuit of what had become a lost cause. Eleanor Marx's obituary of her father paraphrases his position: 'He said [the

Jenny Marx in later life.

International's] work is done, we must not outlive ourselves and fall ignobly to pieces; the end must be voluntary and decent.'[36] Opinions differed about how 'voluntary and decent' it really was. Marx, however – true to form in a sense (for he was good at not seeing things through to completion) – failed to make significant inroads into volumes II and III of *Capital*. Even Engels, after Marx's death in 1883, expressed shock at how far Marx had been from completing it. It is not, to reiterate, that Marx stopped working. He continued to work prodigiously, obsessively. In Engels's words:

> For a man who examined everything to discover its historical origin and the conditions of its development, naturally every

single question gave rise to a series of new questions. Ancient history, agronomics, Russian and American landowning relationships, geology, etc., were studied in particular in order to make the section on ground rent more complete than any previous treatment. He read all the Germanic and Romance languages with ease and then learnt Old Slavonic, Russian, and Serbian.[37]

(The study of the evolution of agriculture in Russia was intended to illuminate Marx's ideas on ground rent in volume III of *Capital* in much the same way that English industrial development provided practical examples of the ideas propounded in volume I.) Engels found among Marx's papers more than two cubic metres of documents containing nothing but Russian statistics, about which he had scribbled 3,000 pages of notes in an execrable, inimitable handwriting that only Engels, seemingly, could read. But Marx's compulsive note-taking betrays a marked involution and turning inwards where once he had resolutely faced outwards; to reiterate yet again, he failed to go through the documents on his desk, determined unto the last to Get It Right.

When Marx's daughter Jenny gave birth to a son in April 1881, he wrote to her the following words:

My 'women folk' hope that the 'newcomer' will increase the 'better half' of humanity; so far as I am concerned at this turning point in history, I favour children of the masculine sex. They have before them the most revolutionary period mankind has ever known. It is bad to be an old man at this time, for an old man can only foresee instead of seeing.

But what nobody could foresee is that Jenny Longuet was to die unexpectedly in January 1883 at the age of 38, just two months before Marx himself. 'I have lived many a sad hour', said Eleanor,

Jenny Marx and daughter Laura.

but none so sad as that. I felt that I was bringing my father his death sentence. I racked my brain all the long anxious way [from Argenteuil to England] to find how I could break the news to him. But I did not need to, my face gave me away. Moor said at once 'our Jennychen is dead.'[38]

And while he was not to know that his grandson, too, would not long survive, it is at least conceivable that Marx died three months later a broken man. But the extent and character of whatever disillusion he underwent needs to be thought about and assessed with reference to the sheer intensity of Marx's political and intellectual commitment, not least in and around the supposed revolutionary *annus mirabilis* of 1848, and certainly during the years of the International and the Commune. Marx, to recapitulate, brought the first volume of *Capital* to completion and to press in 1867 not despite the demands the International made upon his time or 'forced upon him', but *because of* what these demands signified: the possibility that his words might have some immediate practical effect. *Pace* Marx's biographer David McLellan (and for that matter Engels too), Marx's intellectual and political work – his works and his work, if you will – rose and fell together, in tandem, after 1872 as before it.

Conclusion

Immediately after finishing *Capital* volume 1 in 1867, Marx wrote the following words in a letter to Siegfried Meyer:

> Well, why didn't I answer [your last letter]? Because I was constantly hovering at the edge of the grave. I therefore had to use every moment when I was able to work to finish my book, to which I have sacrificed health, happiness and family. I trust that this explanation needs no postscript. I have to laugh at the so-called 'practical' men and their wisdom. If one chose to be an ox, one could of course turn one's back to the sufferings of mankind and look after one's own skin. But I should really have considered myself impractical if I had 'checked out' without completely finishing my book, at least in manuscript form.[1]

These are words to ponder. Not only did Marx wish, according to Paul Lafargue's *Reminiscences*, 'to place [his] knowledge at the service of humanity'; he thought about this knowledge itself in an altogether distinctive way.

'I am working madly through the nights,' Marx wrote in 1857 to Engels, 'so that before the deluge I shall at least have the outlines clear.'[2] This may be one of the most extraordinary statements about theorizing ever made. It does not simply rerun the idiom of its source statement, Louis XIV's notorious but oddly complacent *après moi, le déluge*. The deluge this time is not, like Louis XIV's, about to happen anyway, but is to the contrary a deluge that *isn't* about to happen in the desired way unless Marx's words hit home and prove their effectiveness. Marx's words are extraordinary not because Marx was alone or unique in devoting his life to a revolutionary cause, or in being galvanized by revolutionary urgency. The merest glance at the wonderland of nineteenth-century revolutionism will indicate otherwise. It is extraordinary because of what Marx thought theorizing could do: it could after all be an Archimedean lever with which to move the world. And whatever we think of the movement it effected, it *did* move the world – though not as Marx would have wanted it to, and not necessarily in a manner of which he would have approved. (The solitary success of a beleaguered Russian Revolution laying claim to his mantle was to Marx the least likely of scenarios.)

But, for all this, the provocation of Marx's claim remains. The unsettling social and political changes through which he lived, and which he had the temerity to pin down with a name – capitalism – can be characterized theoretically in such a way that theory itself will be not just 'descriptive' or 'prescriptive' but actually premonitory. It will then stimulate further revolutionary change of a still more fundamental kind. 'What earlier century', Marx had asked in the *Manifesto of the Communist Party*, 'had even a presentiment that such productive forces slumbered in the lap of social labour?' His question deserves to be extended to cover Marx himself as a theorist. Who among Marx's precursors had ever made such exalted claims about the province and purchase of theory? Who 'had even a presentiment' that theory, once it is geared with and meshed into the prospects of revolutionary change, can become the catalyst that could make all the difference to its outcome?

Theory, to be sure, is no demiurge, sweeping all before it. It cannot create dissatisfaction or resentment, cannot engender the desire for fundamental change. But it does not need to do this. What theory can do is channel discontent into worthwhile

The last photo of Marx, taken in Algiers in 1882.

directions, guard against blind alleys and false friends, and reground struggle. Theory need not operate at the expense of agency but at its behest. The working class, Marx's proletariat, can be shown and must be shown how and why it has come into existence, why it is suffering as much as it is suffering, and why its suffering takes the form it does. The working class must in this way be 'taught the secret of its own existence' but not as an insight handed down from on high in the manner of the Mosaic tables. The working class must itself penetrate the 'secret' of its own placement, its role, its task, its agenda, its agency.

Theory properly so-called could thus speak *to* people, not at them – which is to say that what usually passes for scholarly objectivity was not among Marx's priorities. Many scholars have exclaimed with some indignation that he 'imported' extraneous value-judgements into what ought to have been a strictly 'factual' process of inquiry. Marx, it must be said by way of riposte, was no mean scholar. But he was also not one to bear the miseries of others without a murmur. He was never remotely 'academic' or withdrawn. From the very outset, he made no secret of his identification with the wretched of the earth, particularly the industrial proletariat, and he developed his theoretical work on the basis of this avowedly political commitment. He never tried to be detached, value-free, neutral or objective in his analyses even if others were importunately and, I must add, misleadingly, to attach the adjective 'scientific' to his endeavours. (Marx himself, as I have argued at length elsewhere, used the word 'scientific' simply to mean 'systematic' or 'rigorous', nothing more.[3]) This partiality or partisanship makes Marx's intellectual impact all the more striking. Despite what later scholars hastened to identify as his biases, he threw down challenges that they could not afford to ignore.

Marx even changed the vocabulary with which such challenges could be advanced and met. Without Marx we would still have had 'revolution' as a word and as a concept, since the French and the Americans had put revolutionary change on the map in the late eighteenth century. Without Marx, we would still have had 'capitalism'; we would even have had 'socialism' and 'communism'. The celebrated opening sentence of the *Manifesto* was designed to call the reader's attention to something already existing, 'the spectre haunting Europe'. It was designed in other words to invoke, not to invent communism. It is no doubt easier to imagine a world without Marx than a world without revolution, capitalism, communism and socialism. But in the world we actually inhabit, these still have to be seen through Marx. He may not have coined any of these terms, but he set his seal decisively on all of them – so much so that right down to the present day it remains impossible to discuss them without bringing Marx into the discussion. Marx was not alone in having advocated revolution, in having believed in the need for drastic change in order to attain human autonomy. But his sense of the tension between the depravity, the betrayal and the promise of capitalism was all his own.

Other general categories that have become stock-in-trade components of later social and political speculation are more clearly Marx's own formulations: proletariat, including dictatorship of the proletariat; class, including class struggle, class warfare and class consciousness; ideology, including what came to be known as false consciousness; alienation, including the fetishism of commodities, so memorably discussed in the first volume of *Capital*; and, most of all, the method that Friedrich Engels termed 'historical materialism' or the 'materialist conception of history'. Marx's central idea that 'the mode of production of material life conditions the social political and intellectual life process in general' has been of monumental importance to the study of history. Without his emphasis on the influence of economic factors, the entire discipline of history, especially economic history, would have taken a radically different direction in the twentieth century. Without Marx's detailed investigations of labour, commodities, value, wages and exploitation, twentieth-century economics, as well as social science and history, might have taken a very different path. On the one hand, the very idea that capitalist society has an unprecedented structure, within which it makes sense to distinguish microeconomic from macroeconomic analysis, is an idea that owes much to Marx. On the other, the far from outmoded idea that this same structure is rent with contradictions and has tendencies towards potentially catastrophic crises is an idea of distinctly Marxian provenance. Without Marx's juxtaposition of base to superstructure we would probably not be speaking of social contradictions at all, but would instead be discussing science, technology, production, labour, the economy and the state – quite an inventory! – along lines very different from those that have become commonplace today.

Marx evidently casts a long shadow. Even in the case of words in the Marxist lexicon that turn out to owe nothing to Marx himself – scientific socialism, for example, is much more the province of Engels, as is imperialism the province of Lenin, or hegemony of Antonio Gramsci – it is Marx's authority that is generally invoked whenever these terms, and a myriad of terms like them, are employed. Similarly, the term Leninism itself is usually prefaced by Marxist- or Marxism-. If one sign or index of a theorist's power is the adjectival status that is awarded his or her name, then Marx has been powerful indeed.

It bears repetition that what stands out most distinctively about Marx is his unsurpassed sense of the huge potential, alongside the actual depravity, of capitalism, and that this double-edged characterization was one that Marx could proffer without either reaching for a moralistic critique or adopting the romantic notion (one that was far from uncommon among his contemporaries) that capitalism and industry had destroyed a pastoral idyll. It is to Marx we owe the insight that under capitalism the capacity to produce expands, and might exceed all known bounds, while

Lenin unveiling a monument to Marx and Engels in Moscow, November 1918.

ownership of the means of production contracts (relatively or absolutely). We are not yet done – particularly now – with the sheer usefulness of this insight into an asymmetry or maladjustment that is not accidental but built-in. It was Marx's distinction of forces from relations of production that enabled him, and may still enable us today, to deny that physical production and material growth depend by their very nature on the maintenance and furthering of capitalism. Just because a capitalism depends (we are told) on the maintenance of a steady rate of growth, it does not follow that the rate of growth in question depends on the maintenance of capitalism. Marx contended that if capitalism is not understood genetically – understood, that is to say, as it arose, when it arose – we have no way of accounting for its historical specificity. Capitalism will then be falsely and uncritically understood as the universal norm and standard by which all earlier modes of production could be judged, and found wanting. Conversely, these earlier modes of production will be, again falsely and uncritically, regarded as though they were nothing but early, immature, faltering, tentative approximations of capitalism itself. Even as a criterion, capitalism is not unassailable, whether or not what Marx called 'revolutionary activity, practical-critical activity' will suffice as its assailant. The chain of causality that undergirds capitalism, according to which human relationships have become phenomena of the market, can in principle (like the crust of custom) be broken. Capitalism, that is to say, has its enabling assumptions, and these in turn have practical effects; should these cease to operate, capitalism could not and – Marx hastened to add – would not persist.

Marx's career as a revolutionist was never crowned with the kind of practical success he hoped and worked for. But its significance does not end here. To see this we must take a broad view. Plato (at least in the *Republic*) had dared to imagine a politics without chattel slavery; Marx dared to visualize a society without wage labour. While twentieth-century developments have chipped away at the kind of wage labour with which Marx was most immediately familiar, they have neither toppled nor sought to dislodge wage labour from its position as a key component of capitalism. To the extent that we can still speak of capitalism and wage labour – and that extent, I take it, is still considerable – Marx to this day has much to teach us.

Until recently, Marx's central conviction that wage labour was one of capitalism's enabling assumptions and that neither the one

The Marx Memorial Library (established 1933), on London's Clerkenwell Green; both Marx and Lenin knew this old radical meeting place well.

nor the other was sacrosanct or essential to human civilization was often regarded as peremptory and over-optimistic. These days nobody can afford to be so sanguine. This is to say that today, more than ever, Marx must be seen as having thrown down the gauntlet – not least by virtue of his insistence that opposition to capitalism, to be effective, must also be theoretically well grounded. What Marx bequeathed to his followers was a revolutionary doctrine and movement, as well as a method of social, economic, political and historical argument. While the combination was nothing if not fertile, it could all the same be argued, of course, that doctrine, method and movement have never yet found their proper mix – if indeed there is a (singular, unitary) proper mix to be found.

To get Marx into perspective we should remember that in early socialist doctrine there is not a word about the proletariat, the class system or revolution. While John Stuart Mill's *Principles of Political Economy* (1848) regarded socialism and communism not as political movements but simply as theories, Marx and Engels's *Manifesto of the Communist Party* (also 1848), as we have seen, identified communism as a movement that would render socialism as a theory and as nothing more than a theory beside the point, utopian in the sense of being impracticable. It was communism, not socialism, that carried with it the idea of revolutionary struggle and human agency. A new and better society could not be wished or legislated into existence by benevolent doctrinaires, but had to await the advent of a politically conscious labour movement.

Years, decades, were to pass before Marx and Engels dropped the 'communist' label and consented to having their cause described as 'socialist'. A politically oriented labour movement that was self-consciously socialist did emerge in Marx's name later in the nineteenth century, by which point socialism – as we saw above – had changed its meaning. Today the word can mean a social or political doctrine or a political movement or system. In view of vthis latitude, it is not surprising that 'socialism' in social science literature often becomes a noun qualified by an adjective – as in utopian socialism, scientific socialism, state socialism, revolutionary socialism, evolutionary socialism, Fabian socialism, democratic socialism, parliamentary socialism or as in actually existing socialism (until recently) or market socialism. Similarly, the adjective 'socialist' can act as a pendant qualifying or characterizing a noun, as in socialist internationalism, socialist economics, socialist realism, or socialist feminism. The lists go on.

Some of those opposed to capitalism expect too much from Marx, however, and they did this even while Marx was still alive. Why didn't he spell out the lineaments of 'his' future society? (This is a question that still agitates students – at least the ones I teach – today.) Marx had an answer, one put most clearly, perhaps, in an 1881 letter to Ferdinand Domela Nieuwenhuis:

> The doctrinal, and necessarily imaginative anticipation of
> the programme of action for a future revolution only diverts

attention from the present struggle. To dream of the imminent destruction of the world inspired the early Christians and gave them the certainty of victory. The scientific understanding of the inevitable and increasingly visible decay of the prevailing social order, the growing hatred of the masses for the old phantoms who are in power, and the simultaneous huge development of the means of production – all that is a guarantee that at the moment when a real proletarian revolution breaks out there will also appear the conditions (certainly far from idyllic) in which it will carry out its most urgent immediate measures.[4]

People, that is to say, will know what to do – or they won't. Marx, who may of course have been guilty, here and elsewhere, of wishful thinking, nevertheless unflinchingly knew what he alone could have known: he knew what *he* had to do. He may not have finished the tasks he had set himself – he may indeed have been good at not finishing these – but he did make a valiant, principled start. What we can say by way of conclusion, Marx himself said in his *Brumaire* (misquoting his beloved *Hamlet*) of the workers' movement: *Brav gewühlt, alter Maulwurf!* – Well grubbed, old mole!

Marx on an East German banknote, a collaboration he would scarcely have relished.

References

Introduction

1 Sheldon Wolin, quoted in Paul Thomas, *Karl Marx and the Anarchists* (London, 1985 and 2010), p. 13; David McLellan, *Karl Marx: His Life and Thought* (New York, 1973), p. 444.
2 For Engels's speech at Marx's graveside see Karl Marx and Frederick Engels, *Marx–Engels Selected Works* (henceforward *MESW*) (Moscow, 1962), vol. II, pp. 167–9; and, in general, Philip S. Foner, ed., *When Karl Marx Died: Comments in 1883* (New York, 1973).
3 Maximilien Rubel and Margaret Manale, *Marx Without Myth* (Oxford, 1975), p. vii.
4 E. J. Hobsbawm, *The History of Marxism*, vol. I: *Marxism in Marx's Day* (Bloomington, IN, 1982), p. 328.
5 McLellan, *Karl Marx*, p. 360.
6 Karl Marx and Frederick Engels, *Selected Correspondence* (henceforward *MESW*) (Moscow, 1975), p. 137; Marx and Engels, *Letters to Americans, 1848–95* (New York, 1969), p. 65.

1 Trier, Bonn, Berlin, Cologne, 1818–43

1 Karl Marx and Frederick Engels, *Collected Works* (henceforward *MECW*) (New York, 1975–), vol. I, pp. 3–9; Loyd D. Easton and Kurt H. Guddat, eds, *Writings of the Young Marx on Philosophy and Society* (New York, 1967), pp. 34–7.
2 *MECW*, I, pp. 10–21; Easton and Guddat, eds, *Writings*, pp. 40–50.
3 Quoted in David McLellan, *Marx before Marxism* (London and

Basingstoke, 1980), p. 71.

4 *MECW*, I, pp. 25–108.

5 David McLellan, *Karl Marx: His Life and Thought* (New York, 1973), p. 443; cf. Engels to Bernstein, 2–3 November 1882, in *MECW*, XLVI, p. 356; and Engels to Schmidt, 5 August 1890, in *MECW*, XLIX, p. 7.

6 *MECW*, I, pp. 109–31; Easton and Guddat, eds, *Writings*, pp. 67–95.

7 *MECW*, I, pp. 132–81; Easton, eds, *Writings*, pp. 143–8.

8 *MECW*, III, pp. 5–129.

9 Karl Marx, *Selected Writings*, ed. David McLellan (Oxford, 1977), pp. 388–91; cf. *MECW*, I, pp. 224–63, 332–58.

10 *MECW*, III, p. 187.

11 Ibid., p. 186.

2 Paris, 1843–5

1 David McLellan, *Karl Marx: His Life and Thought* (New York, 1973), p. 97.

2 *MECW*, III, pp. 192–206; p. 168; Loyd D. Easton and Kurt H. Guddat, eds, *Writings of the Young Marx on Philosophy and Society* (New York, 1967), pp. 338–58.

3 *MECW*, III, pp. 153–4.

4 Ibid., p. 164.

5 Ibid., p. 168; Karl Marx, *Early Writings*, ed. Lucio Colletti (Harmondsworth, 1975), p. 234.

6 *MECW*, III, pp. 199, 204.

7 Ibid., p. 279; Karl Marx, trans. Martin Milligan, *Economic and Philosophic Writings of 1844* (Moscow, 1961), p. 80.

8 Karl Marx, trans. Ben Fowkes, *Capital*, vol. I (London and Harmondsworth, 1976), pp. 283–4.

9 *MECW*, III, p. 276; Marx, *Economic and Philosophic Writings of 1844*, p. 75.

10 *MECW*, III, p. 276; Marx, *Economic and Philosophic Writings of 1844*, pp. 74–5.

11 Karl Marx, *Selected Writings*, ed. David McLellan (Oxford, 1977), p. 134.

12 *MECW*, III, p. 272; Marx, *Economic and Philosophic Writings of 1844*, p. 70.

3 Brussels, 1845–9

1 Quoted in Jerrold Siegel, *Marx's Fate* (Princeton, NJ, 1978), p. 138.
2 Quoted in David McLellan, *Karl Marx: His Life and Thought* (New York, 1973), pp. 452–3.
3 Karl Marx and Friedrich Engels, trans. Salo Ryanavskaya, *The German Ideology* (Moscow, 1965), p. 37.
4 Karl Marx, trans. Terrell Carver, *Later Political Writings* (Cambridge, 1996), p. 18; Marx and Engels, *German Ideology*, p. 38.
5 Zawar Hanfi, trans. and ed., *The Fiery Brook: Selected Writings of Ludwig Feuerbach* (New York, 1975), p. 157.
6 Marx and Engels, *German Ideology*, p. 47; Marx, *Later Political Writings*, p. 13.
7 *MECW*, III, p. 280.
8 Letter to J. W. Schweitzer, in Karl Marx, *The Poverty of Philosophy* (New York, 1973), pp. 194–202.
9 Karl Marx, *Selected Writings*, ed. David McLellan (Oxford, 1977), p. 134.
10 Ibid., p. 212.
11 Marx, *Later Political Writings*, p. 13.
12 Jacques Derrida, trans. Peggy Kamuf, *Spectres of Marx* (New York and London, 1994).
13 Marx, *Later Political Writings*, p. 1.
14 Malcolm Bull, 'The Ecstasy of Philistinism', *New Left Review*, 219 (September–October 1996), pp. 26–7; Paul Thomas, 'Seeing is Believing: Marx's *Manifesto*, Derrida's Apparition', in *The Communist Manifesto Now: The Socialist Register 1998*, ed. Colin Leys and Leo Panitch (Pontypool, Monmouthshire, 1998), pp. 205–17.
15 Marx, *Later Political Writings*, p. 4.
16 Ibid., p. 5.
17 Ibid., p. 4.
18 Ibid., p. 11.
19 Marx and Engels, *German Ideology*, p. 37.

4 London, 1849–83

1 Quoted in David McLellan, *Karl Marx: His Life and Thought* (New York, 1973), p. 453.

2 Ibid., pp. 454–66.

3 Ibid., pp. 268–9.

4 Yvonne Kapp, *Eleanor Marx*, vol. I: *Family Life* (New York, 1973), p. 34.

5 Jerrold Siegel, *Marx's Fate* (Princeton, NJ, 1978), pp. 250–56.

6 Kapp, *Eleanor Marx*, vol. I, p. 36.

7 Siegel, *Marx's Fate*, p. 269; McLellan, *Karl Marx*, p. 267.

8 McLellan, *Karl Marx*, p. 456.

9 Ibid., p. 415.

10 Kapp, *Eleanor Marx*, vol. I, p. 36.

11 McLellan, *Karl Marx*, pp. 357–8.

12 Ibid., p. 331.

13 Ibid., p. 415.

14 Ibid., p. 417.

15 For a discussion, see Terrell Carver, *Frederick Engels: His Life and Thought* (London, 1989), pp. 161–71.

16 Karl Marx, *Later Political Writings*, trans. and ed. Terrell Carver (Cambridge, 1996), p. 117.

17 Barrington Moore Jr, *Social Origins of Dictatorship and Democracy: Lord and Peasant in the Making of the Modern World* (Boston, MA, 1966).

18 *MESC*, p. 96.

19 *MECW*, III, pp. 280–81.

20 Ibid., p. 281.

21 Karl Marx, *Selected Writings*, ed. David McLellan (Oxford, 1977), p. 381; cf. Paul Thomas, *Marxism and Scientific Socialism* (London, 2008), pp. 142–3.

22 Karl Marx, trans. Ben Fowkes, *Capital*, vol. I (London and Harmondsworth, 1976), p. 236.

23 Marx, *Selected Writings*, p. 379.

24 Marx, *Capital*, vol. I, p. 165.

25 Ibid., p. 166; cf. David Harvey, *A Companion to Marx's Capital* (London, 2010), pp. 79–334.

26 Marx, *Capital*, vol. I, p. 163.

27 Marx, *Selected Writings*, pp. 388–91.

28 Marc Bloch, *Feudal Society*, vol. II: *Social Classes and Political Organization*, trans. L. A. Manion (Chicago, IL, 1964), pp. 353–4. I am grateful to Geraint Parry for first alerting me to the importance of this passage.

29 Marx, *Capital*, vol. I, p. 280; Harvey, *A Companion to Marx's Capital*, p. 107.

30 Marx, *Capital*, vol. I, pp. 450–51; Harvey, *A Companion to Marx's Capital*, p. 175, cf. pp. 256–7.

31 Karl Marx, *Early Writings*, ed. Lucio Colletti (Harmondsworth, 1975), p. 137; *MESC*, p. 65.

32 Marx, 'The Critique of the Gotha Programme', in *MESW*, II, pp. 546, 542.

33 Quoted in Paul Thomas, *Karl Marx and the Anarchists* (London, 1985 and 2010), p. 285.

34 Ibid., pp. 333–6.

35 McLellan, *Karl Marx*, p. 456.

36 Ibid., pp. 455–6.

37 Werner Blumenberg, *Karl Marx: An Illustrated History* (London, 1998), p. 153.

38 McLellan, *Karl Marx*, p. 450.

Conclusion

1 Quoted in Jerrold Siegel, *Marx's Fate* (Princeton, NJ, 1978), p. 387.

2 Karl Marx and Friedrich Engels, *Marx-Engels Werke* (Berlin, 1966), vol. XXIX, p. 225; quoted in Paul Thomas, *Karl Marx and the Anarchists* (London, 1985 and 2010), p. 12.

3 See Paul Thomas, *Marxism and Scientific Socialism: From Engels to Althusser* (London, 2008), esp. pp. 2–67.

4 Marx to Ferdinand Domela Niewenhuis, 22 February 1881, *MESC*, p. 410.

Further Reading

Marx's earlier writings attained 'canonical' status only belatedly. The writings that an immensely productive Engels introduced and disseminated between Marx's death in 1883 and his own in 1895, apart from *Capital*, include only one from before 1847, the short, aphoristic and cryptic 'Theses on Feuerbach', written (but not published) in 1845. The others were *The Poverty of Philosophy*, 'Wage-Labour and Capital' and the 'Speech on Free Trade', all from 1847; *The Communist Manifesto* of 1848; the *Eighteenth Brumaire of Louis Bonaparte* (1852); the 'Speech to the Cologne Jury' of 1853; *The Civil War in France* (1871); and 'The Critique of the Gotha Programme' (written but not published in 1875). Many conclusions were derived from these and these alone concerning what academics as well as political stalwarts termed 'Marxism' and/or (Engels's term) 'Historical Materialism', even though these writings in time ceased to be, and ceased to be considered to be, the sole nucleus on which judgements could or should be based. With the later addition of other writings that augmented the corpus, its centre of gravity shifted. Most 'Selections' from Marx's writings published since the 1960s – their number is legion – would also (rightly) include materials from 'On "The Jewish Question"' of 1843; *The Holy Family* (1844); the *Economic and Philosophic Manuscripts of 1844*; the manuscripts that have come down to us as the 1842 and 1844 *Critique(s) of Hegel's 'Philosophy of Right'*; the *German Ideology* (1845–6); *The Class Struggles in France* (1850); and the *Grundrisse* (1857–8).

The most complete edition in English of Marx's writings is the *Marx–Engels Collected Works* (*MECW*), initiated in 1975 by Lawrence & Wishart (London) and International Publishers (New York). This edition, while more authoritative and easier to use than any other, is unlikely to be the most accessible to the general reader, who is referred also to the Marx

Library begun in 1973 by Allen Lane's Penguin Books in collaboration with the New Left Review in the UK, and by Random House / Vintage in conjunction with Monthly Review Press in the USA. The series includes *Early Writings*, ed. Lucio Colletti; *The Revolutions of 1848*, ed. David Fernbach; *Surveys From Exile*, ed. David Fernbach; *Grundrisse*, ed. Martin Nicolaus; *The First International and After*, ed. David Fernbach; and the three volumes of *Capital*, in a new translation by Ben Fowkes. Another valuable resource is provided by the Cambridge Texts in the History of Political Thought, edited by Raymond Geuss and Quentin Skinner, which include Marx's *Early Political Writings*, ed. Joseph O' Malley, and his *Later Political Writings*, ed. Terrell Carver (Cambridge UP, 1996). By now, the once-standard two-volume 1962 Moscow / Foreign Languages Publishing House edition of Marx and Engels's *Selected Works* (*MESW*) needs complementing. The Norton *Marx–Engels Reader*, ed. Robert M. Tucker, is unreliable and best avoided. More useful selections include David McLellan's edition of Marx's *Selected Writings* (1977), along with the still-useful and well-chosen *Selected Writings in Sociology and Social Philosophy*, ed. T. B. Bottomore and Maximilien Rubel (Penguin, 1970; McGraw-Hill, 1964); T. B. Bottomore's 1963 edition of Marx's *Early Writings*; Loyd D. Easton and Kurt Guddat's *Writings of the Young Marx* (Anchor/Doubleday, 1967).

Pride of place among English-language biographies of Marx still goes to Isaiah Berlin's *Karl Marx: His Life and Environment*, originally published in 1939. Its fourth edition (Oxford, 1997) contains an invaluable 'Guide to Further Reading' by Terrell Carver, which is unhesitatingly to be recommended. David McLellan's *Karl Marx: His Life and Thought* (Harper and Row, 1974) is more up-to-date, thus more comprehensive, than Berlin's – McLellan was a student of Berlin's – but all the same less memorable. (I still remember where I was when I read Berlin on Marx for the first time.) Maximilien Rubel and Margaret Manale's *Marx Without Myth* (Blackwell, 1975), Boris Nicholaevsky and Otto Maechen-Helfen's *Karl Marx, Man and Fighter* (Penguin, 1975), and Jerrold Siegel's *Marx's Fate* (Princeton UP, 1978) are all useful. Some readers have found Francis Wheen's more recent popular biography, *Karl Marx* (1999), refreshingly non-academic. These and others should perhaps turn to Werner Blumenberg's *Karl Marx: An Illustrated Biography* (Verso, 1998); W. A. Suchting, *Marx: An Introduction* (New York UP, 1983); and Allen Wood, *Karl Marx* (Routledge, 1981).

Critical commentaries on Marx abound; recommendations are necessarily subjective. Shlomo Avineri's *The Social and Political Thought of Karl Marx* (Cambridge UP, 1970) and George Lichtheim's *Marxism: A Historical and Critical Study* (Praeger, 1965) are excellent general surveys that have stood the test of time, as has the (multi-authored) *Cambridge Companion to Marx*, ed. Terrell Carver (1991). Recommended studies of individual works or specific periods include David McLellan's *The Young Hegelians and Karl Marx* (Praeger, 1966), and *Marx Before Marxism* (Harper, 1970). Marx's manuscript(s) known as the *Critique(s) of Hegel's 'Philosophy of Right'* have been ably edited by Joseph O'Malley for Cambridge University Press (1970). And while István Mezáros's *Marx's Theory of Alienation* (Merlin Press, 1970; Harper, 1972), the best book on the *Economic and Philosophic Manuscripts* of 1844, is tough going at first, so are the *Manuscripts* themselves, and these too will repay the effort expended. Marshall Berman's *All That is Solid Melts into Air* (Simon & Schuster, 1982) contains a short but spirited interpretation of the *Manifesto of the Communist Party*, but the best survey of the political and philosophical background to the *Manifesto* may be Gareth Stedman Jones's painstaking 'Introduction' to the Penguin Classics edition (2002), pp. 3–187. Another foundational text, Marx's 'Introduction' to *A Contribution to the Critique of Political Economy*, is ably and arrestingly interpreted by Terrell Carver in his *Marx's Social Theory* (Oxford UP, 1982). Paul Thomas, *Karl Marx and the Anarchists* (Routledge, 1985 and 2010), deals with Marx as a revolutionary activist as well as a revolutionary theorist; his *Marxism and Scientific Socialism* (Routledge, 2008) is concerned with what Marx meant and did not mean by 'science'.

Acknowledgements

My deepest thanks go to my wife, Mimy Ng, and my son, George Thomas. My grateful thanks are also due to Marshall Berman, who helped get this project off the ground, and to Martin Jay, who was kind enough to read an earlier version of the entire manuscript and whose comments helped me enormously in its revision. Thanks also to Terrell Carver, Wendy Brown and the late Norman Jacobson for their encouragement, and to the Department of Political Science and the Committee on Research at the University of California, Berkeley, for their support.

Photo Acknowledgements

The author and publishers wish to express their thanks to the below sources of illustrative material and/or permission to reproduce it. (Locations uncredited in the captions are also given below.)

From Karl Marx, *Das Kapital* (Hamburg, 1867): p. 18; Musée d'Orsay, Paris (painting by G. Courbet, 1865): p. 88; Museo Napoleonico, Rome (painting by F. X. Winterhalter, 1855): p. 128; Museum of K. Marx and F. Engels of the Institute of Marxism-Leninism of the Central Committee of the CPSU, Moscow (painting by Y. Sapiro, 1961): p. 63; photos courtesy Marx Memorial Library, London: pp. 6, 9, 48, 108, 112, 118, 121, 140, 160, 161, 163, 167.